Then I WILL GO

Obedience, Victory, and God's Providence
LESSONS FROM THE BOOK OF ESTHER

Authors

Ali Shaw • Courtney Cohen • Jaime Hilton

Kat Lee • Kelli LaFram • Kelly R. Baker • Sabrina Gogerty

Hellomornings.org

TABLE OF CONTENTS

THE NEW Hellomornings BIBLE STUDY METHOD .V

SHARE THE STUDY VII

The Big Bible Study Idea List . . . . *viii*

Read And Write . . . . *viii*

Respond. . . . . *ix*

Research . . . . *.x*

Ready To Dive In? . . . . *xi*

INTRODUCTION 2

WEEK ONE 4

Week 1, Day 1: 2 Chronicles 36:11-21 4

Week 1, Day 2: 2 Chronicles 36:22-23; Ezra 6:1-5 and 14-15 6

Week 1, Day 3: Esther 1:1-4 8

Week 1, Day 4: Esther 1:5-9 10

Week 1, Day 5: Esther 1:10-15 12

WEEK TWO 14

Week 2, Day 1: Esther 1:16-22 14

Week 2, Day 2: Esther 2:1-11. 16

Week 2, Day 3: Esther 2:12-18 18

Week 2, Day 4: Esther 2:19-23 20

Week 2, Day 5: Esther 3:1-6 22

WEEK THREE 24

Week 3, Day 1: Esther 3:7-11. 24

Week 3, Day 2: Esther 3:12-15 26

Week 3, Day 3: Esther 4:1-5 28

Week 3, Day 4: Esther 4:6-11. 30

Week 3, Day 5: Esther 4:12-17 32

WEEK FOUR 34

Week 4, Day 1: Esther 5:1-8 34

Week 4, Day 2: Esther 5:9-14. 36

Week 4, Day 3: Esther 6:1-9 38

Week 4, Day 4: Esther 6:10-14 40

Week 4, Day 5: Esther 7:1-6 42

WEEK FIVE **44**

Week 5, Day 1: Esther 7:7-10 . . . . *44*

Week 5, Day 2: Esther 8:1-7 . . . . *46*

Week 5, Day 3: Esther 8:8-14 . . . . *48*

Week 5, Day 4: Esther 8:15-17 . . . . *50*

Week 5, Day 5: Esther 9:1-10 . . . . *52*

WEEK SIX **54**

Week 6, Day 1: Esther 9:11-15 . . . . *54*

Week 6, Day 2: Esther 9:16-22 . . . . *56*

Week 6, Day 3: Esther 9:23-28 . . . . *58*

Week 6, Day 4: Esther 9:29-32 . . . . *60*

Week 6, Day 5: Esther 10:1-3 . . . . *62*

CONCLUSION **64**

ABOUT THE AUTHORS **65**

MAPS **67**

THE NEW Hellomornings BIBLE STUDY METHOD

We (The HelloMornings Team) are SO excited to share this new Bible study method with you!

The heart behind the method is "For Every Woman in Every Season." Whether you have 5 minutes or 50 minutes every morning, the HelloMornings study method can adapt to your schedule. We designed it so that a new believer won't feel overwhelmed and a seasoned Bible study student can dive deep into each passage.

We had three main goals in creating this method:

1. TO BUILD YOUR HABIT

Because building a daily God time habit is at the core of HelloMornings, we want to make sure you never feel overwhelmed with each day's study. If you only have 5 minutes, you can read the passage, write the verse and respond in a written prayer. If you have more time, you can dig deeper with one, two or all of the study "action steps." And if you want to go even deeper (or stretch the study out to a Saturday or Sunday) we are including group of study ideas in the front of the ebook so you'll always have a treasure trove of options to choose from.

2. TO BUILD YOUR GROUP

Our second goal was to create a method that encourages group interaction. Groups are integral to what we do here at HelloMornings. They are a way to build community, stay accountable to growth and learn from different perspectives.

But it's hard to find a group where everyone is at the same level of studying Scripture. That means with most Bible studies, some group members feel overwhelmed while others feel bored. Our goal is to bridge that gap and create content that not only fits any schedule, but also fits any level of study.

The beauty of this is that someone in your group who is brand new to the faith can daily dive into the same scriptures as a group leader who has been studying for decades. And the way we have formatted the content allows for each to learn and share in whatever way God is leading them so everyone can feel they have something to contribute, if they choose.

3. TO BUILD YOUR ROUTINE

In order to be the "hands and feet of Jesus," we need to:

1. Know Him—(God)
2. Understand His purpose for our lives—(Plan)
3. Follow His leading—(Move)

These are the core habits of HelloMornings.

God. Plan. Move.

Time with God is essential. And we believe that God has a purpose for each one of our lives. We also believe that He even has a purpose for each of our days. There are people He may want you to encourage today or ways He wants you to take action.

That is why we Plan. We want our daily planning to be done with His purposes in mind. Each daily worksheet has space for just a few of the most important tasks. Prayerfully planning is more powerful than any fancy productivity system because only God knows our heart, our purpose and our circumstances.

Finally, it's time to Move. This doesn't need to be a 3-mile run or a 25-minute workout. We simply want to be "fit for our calling"—i.e. have the energy to walk out the plan toward our purpose. If God has things He'd like us to do today, it's our responsibility to have the energy to do them. He does not give us more than we can handle.

For some, this might be simply drinking a morning glass of water. For others, it might be a short workout and for others it might be a healthy breakfast. The goal is just to do what we can to have the energy to respond to whatever God is calling us to each day. Kind of like an athlete makes sure to eat a good breakfast before a game so she has the energy to play well.

God. Plan. Move.

It doesn't need to take a long time. It could be as simple as a 5-minute routine of reading the daily passage, jotting down a few tasks and drinking a glass of water. Or it could be longer and more customized to your life.

Ultimately, we just want to start each day with the One who gave us all our days. And we want to plan our lives with the One who gives us our lives. And we want to Move wherever He may lead.

To a life well lived for the good of others and the glory of God,

The HelloMornings Team

SHARE THE STUDY

Will you consider helping us spread the word?

If you're in a HelloMornings group, invite all your group members to upgrade from the basic reading plan to this full study. It is well worth the price of a latte to study scripture deeply for 6 weeks and build a solid morning routine.

If you don't have a HelloMornings group, gather some friends together, send them to *HelloMornings.org/shop* to grab a copy of the study and spend the next 6 weeks journeying together! It's so much more fun and impactful when we learn and grow in community.

WAYS TO HELP OTHERS:

Use the hashtag *#HelloMornings* on Twitter or Instagram.

Share what you're learning on Facebook and link to *HelloMornings.org*

Tell your friends! Text, email or invite them to join you the next time you see them.

GET ALL THE RESOURCES:

We want to equip you to build a brilliant, God centered morning routine that leaves you feeling refueled and ready for action each day.

If you're not already on our email list, visit *HelloMornings.org* to download our free resources and receive our inspiring and idea-filled newsletter.

THE BIG BIBLE STUDY IDEA LIST

Each day of a HelloMornings study is filled with passages to read, a verse to write and plenty of action steps to take. But if you're ready to dive even deeper or you want to stretch our 5 day a week studies into 7 days, this list is the perfect way for you to add "tools" to your Bible study tool belt.

If you finish the study for the day and have more time, simply refer back to this "Big Bible Study Idea List" to select a few ways to dive even deeper into the passage you've been reading.

The best thing about this list is that it can be used on ANY section of scripture. So, if you want to do a study on 1 Corinthians 13 or look up all the verses on Faith, just use this list to build your own Bible study!

We want to equip you to study the Bible deeply regardless of whether you have a Bible study guide you're going through at the time or not. Try out each of these "tools" and add them to your Bible study "tool belt!"

READ AND WRITE

Ways to study scripture and dig deep into one passage.

READ

Simply read the passage. You can read it in your head, read out loud, read thoughtfully and slow, read in another translation.

WRITE

Honestly, this is my favorite way to start each morning. I *love* writing out scripture. There's something about the process of handwriting that both wakes me up and allows me to really marinate in the passage. It's also incredibly meaningful to have notebooks filled with handwritten scripture.

IDENTIFY KEY VERSES

In the passage you're reading, which verse holds the nugget of wisdom. Which verses explain the transformation of the main characters. Which verses speak most deeply to you in the season you're in right now?

HIGHLIGHT, UNDERLINE, BRACKET, CIRCLE, JOT

In this digital age, there is something therapeutic about words on a paper page and a pack of highlighters or colored pencils. I always loved looking at my grandmothers Bible filled with highlights, underlines, notes and circles.

Take time to circle commands, underline truths or highlight key verses in your favorite shade of pink. Bible study can be fun and colorful!

OBSERVE

Let your inner Nancy Drew loose. Uncover the 5 W's of the passage. Who, What, When, Where, Why and (don't forget) How. It's amazing how much we can learn from just naming the different elements of a passage or story.

ILLUSTRATE

In the margins of your Bible, or on a HelloMornings worksheet, get creative! Design word art focusing on a key point. Sketch the setting, characters or theme.

OUTLINE

Feeling more cerebral than creative? Outline the story or teaching. Highlight the main points and the sub-points to develop a greater understanding of where the author was coming from and what he was trying to communicate.

PERSONAL PARAPHRASE

Sometimes we learn best by teaching. Imagine you had to share the heart of the passage with a group of friends or a class of children, how would you paraphrase it? Or paraphrase it by incorporating your story into it and the things God has done in your life. You could even paraphrase it by simply incorporating your name in everywhere it has a generic pronoun.

QUESTIONS

Got questions? Just write them down. You can answer them later. Don't let your questions keep you from getting through the passage. Imagine you could interview the author, what would you ask?

RESPOND

A great way to dig deeper into scripture is to as a few simple questions. You can think about the answers as you read or you can write down your responses on the HelloMornings worksheet or in your own journal.

The Bible truly comes alive when we consider and pray about how God wants us to apply it to our own lives.

QUESTIONS TO CONSIDER:
- What does this say about God?
- What does this say about the church?
- What does this say about me?
- What truths are in this passage?
- Does this passage lead me to confess anything in prayer?

- What should I pray?
- What actions should I take?
- How can today be different because of this passage?
- What are some journaling questions?
- What is the lesson from this passage?
- Which key verse should I memorize this week?

RESEARCH

There is so much to be learned on every page of scripture. But sometimes we can take our study to a new level when we start flipping the pages and learning the "story behind the story."

Here are a few things you can research about the passage you are studying.

AUTHOR

Who wrote this passage? What do we know about him and how he fits into the story of the Bible? What were his circumstances? Why did he write it? Who was he writing to? Where was he when he wrote it? What had God done in his life to compel him to write this passage?

BACKGROUND

What was the background of the passage? What story or theme was introduced in previous verses or chapters of the book?

AUDIENCE

Who was the audience that the author was writing to? Why was it written to them? How do you think they responded to it? How would you have responded?

CONTEXT: CULTURAL, HISTORICAL, GRAMMATICAL

What was happening in history at the time the passage was written? What was the culture in which it was written like? How did the culture or the historical circumstances influence the author? Are there any grammatical rhythms or clues identifying or strengthening the authors meaning or ultimate intent?

CROSS REFERENCE

If you have a Bible with cross references (or using an online resource), look up all the verses associated with the passage. What can you learn from them and how do they influence the text?

COMMENTARIES

Read the commentary in your Bible, commentary books or at a trusted online source to gain even more insight into the passage.

TRANSLATIONS

Read the passage in multiple translations. How do they differ? How are they the same? What new truths can you glean from the variety of perspectives?

MAPS

Are there any maps in your Bible or online related to the passage you're studying? Follow the journey of the main characters. Look up modern day pictures of the locations. Research how long their journeys may have taken or any obstacles they may have encountered in their travels (culturally or geographically).

WORD STUDY (ORIGINAL LANGUAGE)

Brush up on your Greek and Hebrew and study the passage in the original language using an interlinear Bible.

READY TO DIVE IN?

Feel free to refer back to this list at any point, but now it's time to dive into the new HelloMornings study.

Here we go...

Cheering you on,

Kat Lee and the *HelloMornings.org* Team

FREE AUDIO VERSION

Email your Amazon receipt to us and get the audio version of this study for free!

Audios@hellomornings.org

Then I WILL GO

Obedience, Victory, and God's Providence
LESSONS FROM THE BOOK OF ESTHER

THE BOOK OF ESTHER IS AN EXCITING STORY beloved by many! If you're already familiar with it, you likely know of the beautiful, courageous queen described in the narrative who has, rightly, inspired countless Christians to love God boldly and bravely. Esther was a Jewish Queen of Persia who bravely approached King Xerxes I (Ahasuerus) and delivered her people from certain annihilation. Her situation was truly unique. But like opening the far back curtain on a stage, a close inspection of her story reveals more than just a beautiful, bold queen. It reveals a powerful, loving God working actively behind the scenes. Yes, Esther was brave, but God's mighty hand of Providence was orchestrating the details to save and give victory to His people through her obedience.

Esther was born a Jewish exile into the Achaemenid Empire, or the First Persian Empire, after the nation of Israel was forced to leave their country following the 6th century B.C. invasion of King Nebuchadnezzar of Babylon. Like we discussed in the introduction to the Hello Mornings Bible study on the Book of Nehemiah, *Rebuilt and Restored, God's Wonderful Work of Renewal*:

> They were subsequently forced to live in exile for 70 years. This was God's act of judgement on His people for their repeated acts of idolatry (see 2 Kings 17). God had warned them as early as Moses' time to continue faithfully obeying God or suffer the consequences (see Deuteronomy 28:45-52), but they were stiff necked and rebellious. It took an exile to a foreign land for the Jews to repent of their idolatry. But during this Babylonian Exile, the Jewish people maintained many aspects of their national culture and lived out a rededicated, repentant worship.

The Babylonian Empire fell to Persia in 539 B.C., when King Cyrus invaded and conquered, establishing the new First Persian Empire. About a year later, Cyrus made a decree in 538 BC stating that exiled Jews could return home to Jerusalem (see Ezra 1) to rebuild the Temple, though many stayed behind in Persia. The Book of Esther takes place roughly 50 years after Cyrus' decree, 40 years after the Temple in Jerusalem had been rebuilt, and 30 years before Nehemiah began rebuilding of the wall in Jerusalem. The book gives us great insight into how the Jews who stayed behind lived in the Persian Empire, but more importantly, this book that never specifically mentions God, shows us His sovereign nature and providential activity.

Though God is the main character behind the scenes, of course, there are other important characters displayed up front. Many people study the Book of Esther with the spotlight on her. We'll definitely look at her in this study, but we'll also look at her cousin, Mordecai, and his faith. Mordecai was highly esteemed in Jewish tradition for his role in saving the Jews. It was at his urging that Esther spoke to Ahasuerus on behalf of her people. Mordecai also refused to honor Haman by bowing down before him. In that kingdom and time, such an act implied showing Haman *divine* honor, which God had commanded the Jews not to do. Like Esther, Mordecai also risked his life in an act of obedience.

Pray with me?

Father, help us to be inspired by both Esther and Mordecai's faith and obedience. Open our eyes to see your hand in preserving your Jewish children through Mordecai's prompting and Esther's brave actions. Let us even see the parallels of how Esther's actions were a foreshadowing of the result of Christ's sacrifice. Like Christ, she was willing to obey even unto death (Philippians 2:8) to save her people. Help us see that through your help and strength, the Jews were victorious over the enemy. Help us remember that through Christ's sacrifice, Jesus was victorious over Satan, and through Jesus' grace, we are victorious over Satan, as well. Thank you for being a God who loves us powerfully, guides us providentially, saves us eternally, and gives us victory! Help us to have faith and determination so that, at your call, no matter the cost, we can say, *"Then I will go."* Amen.

Ali

NOTE TO READER: *In this study, an author may mention Jewish tradition, Midrash, and so forth. While interesting and sometimes helpful, it is important to note that information from Jewish Midrash and other commentaries, traditions, as well as the Apocrypha, etc., should not be given the same authority as the infallible Word of God.*

WEEK 1, DAY 1: 2 CHRONICLES 36:11-21

WE'VE ALL SEEN IT BEFORE and maybe have experienced it firsthand. The child who didn't listen to wise instruction, the teen who needed to learn everything "the hard way," or the celebrity who fell from stardom after a scandal surfaced have all learned this same fact: rebellion has consequences.

Early in Jewish history, the Israelites had demanded a person-king, rejecting God as king. First was King Saul. After his disobedience (1 Samuel 13:11-15), God promised the kingdom to David, son of Jesse, whose offspring would rule forever (2 Samuel 7:12-16, Matthew 1:1-17). Solomon, David's son, reigned next and built the temple in Jerusalem. But under the reign of his son, Rehoboam, the unified kingdom was split in two: Judah, which had a mix of godly and evil kings, and Israel, whose line of evil kings led the people deep into idolatry. Through alliances with Israel, the kings of Judah followed Israel's idolatrous example.

In today's passage, we see how Esther and other Jews came to be in Persia. We learn of the siege and captivity of Judah, a story of rebellion and consequences. Verses 11 through 16 are so sad! God had always been so faithful and generous to His children, yet they did not follow Him, nor turn to Him with repentant faith immediately after they had strayed. Instead, they brushed God aside in nasty rebellion. They despised His words and scoffed at His prophets until He was provoked to carry out a plan to save them from themselves.

Yet through it all, God was involved. Though it may not have appeared so to the non-observant onlooker, Providence was carried out when, during the third and final siege in 587 B.C., Nebuchadnezzar entered Jerusalem and destroyed the temple, city gates, and walls. God would use this defeat and the subsequent Babylonian exile to purify Israel of their idolatry.

Yes, rebellion has consequences. When we repent, God can use those consequences to bring us closer into fellowship with Him, if we allow it. The story of the capture of Jerusalem can be our reminder to search our hearts for rebellion against Him. If (when) we find it, we have two options: *don't* or *do* turn to God. If we continue in our rebellion, we can be sure that our sovereign Father will deal with us as He sees fit (Hebrews 12:3-11). When we run to His open arms with repentant hearts, we can be assured that He will forgive (Isaiah 1:18, 55:6-7, and Luke 15:10). Praise God!

— **KEY VERSE** —

The LORD, the God of their fathers, sent persistently to them by his messengers, because he had compassion on his people and on his dwelling place. (2 Chronicles 36:15)

Hello mornings

God. Plan. Move.

READ : 2 Chronicles 36:11-21
WRITE : 2 Chronicles 36:15

REFLECT :
- What does this passage say about God? What is He saying to you through this story?
- Read more about the Babylonian invasion: 2 Kings 24:17 through 2 Kings 25:21.
- Two reasons are given for the captivity. What are they and how are they both rebellion?
- Why did the land need its Sabbaths? See Leviticus 25:2-7.
- Ask God to show you any rebellion in your heart. Ask for forgiveness with a repentant heart, and thank Him for forgiving you.

RESPOND :

PLAN TIME

THINGS TO DO (3-5 MAX) :

KEY EVENTS TODAY :

MOVE TIME

MORNING WATER ☐

B : _____
L : _____
D : _____

SNACK :

SIMPLE WORKOUT ☐

MY YOUNGEST DAUGHTER ENJOYS LEGO SETS. It's really incredible how a detailed final model is built from tiny, individual squares. During the process, units are put together into oddly shaped chunks. Without patience and master plans at hand, it's hard to see how these seemingly random pieces could come together in just the right way, in the right order, to make a "masterpiece."

Today's reading builds on yesterday's; we're given more pieces to the background story of the Book of Esther. We begin to see a design built by the hand of Providence. Only God could have set the historical timeline and orchestrated the details and events so perfectly to accomplish His will in saving His people. The prophecies of Isaiah 45:1 and Jeremiah 29:10 are fulfilled. Cyrus the Great, already King of Persia for 20 years, defeated the Babylonians in 539 B.C. and inherited the exiled Jews. During *"the first year of Cyrus"* in 538 B.C. (2 Chronicles 36:22), he decreed that they could return home to rebuild the Jerusalem Temple. His decree came at the end of the prophesied 70 year captivity, which had begun during the first of Nebuchadnezzar's invasions around 608/605 B.C. and lasted until the decree in 538 B.C.*

The Persian Empire operated differently from the Assyrian and Babylonian Empires that had ruled before. Rather than uprooting conquered peoples and incorporating them into their kingdoms, they let captives remain home to serve under local governors to prevent revolts. God used this important "Lego piece" detail in a providential way to get His people home.

God also used the Persians' religion to accomplish His will. One might believe Cyrus' heart was softened toward God since he dismissed the Jews to build a temple. But interestingly, the term "God of heaven" does not point to Cyrus' belief in God, but showed the nature of Zoroastrianism, the monotheistic yet inclusive faith he practiced. In another twist, temples weren't important to Zoroastrian faith! These details are more building blocks of God's plan.

Many Jews returned home to rebuild the temple but the work was later halted by their enemies and an order from King Artaxerxes. (See Ezra 4) Our sovereign God stepped in and put the pieces together when King Darius I searched and found instructions and the decree and ordered for them to be enforced. All of this assures us that only God manages the timeline and details of history and His hand of Providence is mighty in caring for all of His children!

— KEY VERSE —

Thus said Cyrus king of Persia, All the kingdoms of the earth has the LORD God of heaven given me; and he has charged me to build him an house in Jerusalem, which is in Judah. (2 Chronicles 36:23a)

*Allowing for differences in ancient and modern calendars, the exile lasted 70 years

GOD TIME

READ : 2 Chronicles 36:22-23; Ezra 6:1-5 and 14-15
WRITE : 2 Chronicles 36:23a

....

....

REFLECT :
- Sovereignty refers to God's position; it is part of His nature. Providence is God's sovereignty in action. Using what you've learned today, take notes on the passages with this in mind.
- On God's sovereignty, see: Prov 21:1, Jeremiah 18:1-8, Daniel 4:35, and Isaiah 46:9-11.
- Read Isaiah 45:1-7. What does this tell us about God? About Cyrus? About mankind?
- How have you seen Providence in your own life?
- Spend time in awe-filled worship, praising God for His sovereignty and providence.

RESPOND :

....

....

....

....

PLAN TIME

THINGS TO DO (3-5 MAX) :

MOVE TIME

MORNING WATER ☐

B : _____
L : _____
D : _____

KEY EVENTS TODAY :

SNACK :

SIMPLE WORKOUT ☐

WEEK 1, DAY 3: ESTHER 1:1-4

"I WANT TO BE A PRINCESS, MOMMY!" My daughter looked at me with longing. I excitedly explained that she actually *was* a princess. Answering her puzzled look, I told her that her Heavenly Father is the King and since she is His daughter, she is a princess. She tried to hide her disappointment and answered softly, "Oh. But I want to be a *real* princess." She didn't see that spiritual exaltation and identity are just as real as, and are more important than, the temporal.

Today we start the Book of Esther. Chronologically, the events recorded in Esther occur between Ezra 6 and 7. King Ahasuerus, son of Darius I, was now king of the powerful Persian Empire, residing in one of its capital cities, the citadel of Susa, in modern day Iran. Known in history as Xerxes I, we see glimpses of his position and personality in the first four verses of Esther 1.

In the third year of his reign, about 483 B.C, when Xerxes was 39 years old, he gave a 180 day banquet for his officials, servants, nobles, governors, and army. His kingdom was strong and Xerxes was mighty, and it seems he enjoyed showing it. For six months, Xerxes showed off. While displaying royal treasure was not unusual (see Isaiah 39:2), Xerxes did it with prideful flair. According to scholars, there were likely about 15,000 people in attendance. Xerxes was proud and powerful

"There is a want in the soul of man which all the wealth of one hundred and twenty-seven provinces cannot supply. ...Money cannot purchase for him peace and pardon. [Xerxes] was as poor as the humblest serf in his dominions in this respect, and far poorer than the poorest of the children of Judah, dispersed through his empire as exiles, but knowing Jehovah."—A.B. Davidson, D.D

Yes! Even the poorest of the poor is rich because of knowing God! Xerxes was laden with treasures and power, yet he was lacking. Like my daughter who wanted to be an earthly princess rather than a heavenly one, Xerxes' focus seemed to be on the temporal. It's important for us to always remember that there is much more to life than what our physical eyes see. Isn't that wonderful? We are promised spiritual riches (Colossians 1:27) and power and might (Acts 1:8, 2 Timothy 2:16), through humbling ourselves (James 4:10) and serving like Jesus Christ (John 13:1-17, Philippians 4:13). The Savior, who gave His life for us, exalts and empowers us!

— KEY VERSE —

While he showed the riches of his royal glory and the splendor and pomp of his greatness for many days, 180 days. (Esther 1:4)

Hello mornings
God. Plan. Move.

READ : Esther 1:1-4
WRITE : Esther 1:4

· ·

· ·

REFLECT :
- What stands out to you from today's passage?
- How do you think Xerxes' personality could set the stage to see Providence in action?
- What can you learn from Ephesians 2:4-6, James 4:10, 1 Peter 5:5-6, and Luke 14-7-11?
- God empowers us! See Habakkuk 3:19, Isaiah 40:29-31, and Ephesians 3:16, 20-21.
- Do you struggle with pride or focusing on the temporal? Use your concordance or an online search to help you find verses for meditation.

RESPOND :

· ·

· ·

· ·

· ·

· ·

PLAN TIME

THINGS TO DO (3-5 MAX) :

KEY EVENTS TODAY :

MOVE TIME

MORNING WATER ☐

B : _____
L : _____
D : _____

SNACK :

SIMPLE WORKOUT ☐

WEEK 1, DAY 4: ESTHER 1:5-9

WE LIVE IN A WORLD WHERE VANITY ABOUNDS. Not to be a downer, but one doesn't have to look around much before you see it. Magazine covers, social media posts, the internet, and pop culture show us ways to look younger, better, more in style, and tell us what's in and what's not. I was recently shocked (not really) to learn that my wall color is outdated because Pinterest told me so. Seriously, we *should* take care of ourselves, our homes, and so on, but when we place excessive importance on things that are empty, worthless, and futile, we're being vain.

Xerxes was a vain man in a vain world. Yesterday, we talked about His powerful position and his great pride. Today we see vanity. The King of Persia gives another banquet, this time a seven day feast for all the people in Susa. And the opulence described in verses 6-8 drips with vanity.

Imagine the scene: the enormous, verdant, garden court is decorated with incredible finery. Cotton curtains are hung and blow in the sultry heat. Guests dressed in their richest attire recline on gold and silver couches, drinking until intoxicated. The atmosphere would have been crowded and noisy, with indulgence to the point of lewd and lascivious behavior.

You and I will likely never be a royal banquet guest, but we will be tempted toward vanity. How can we make sure our motives aren't vain when we're taking care of ourselves, making a home for our families, or simply living a fun and interesting life? I love this advice:

"When you are tempted to any vanity—set the blessed Redeemer before you, consider His example, and ask yourself, 'How would Jesus, my Lord and Master, have acted in such a case? Would He have spent His time upon such trifles? Would He have spoken such and such; or done this or the other thing, which I am solicited to do? And shall I give way to that which would be a manifest deviation from His holy example? God forbid!'"—Theologian, John Fawcett (1739—1817)

When our hearts are in the right place, focused on serving God and not ourselves, we find a sober-mindedness that guides our actions. We don't have to be like Xerxes, conforming to worldly pleasure and focusing on riches that would some day rot away. All that remains today of Susa is a few heaps, but spiritual riches are eternal. (Matthew 6:19-21). Praise God that we can know and with His help do better!

— **KEY VERSE** —

Do not be conformed to this world, but be transformed by the renewal of your mind, that by testing you may discern what is the will of God, what is good and acceptable and perfect. (Romans 12:2)

Hello mornings
God. Plan. Move.

GOD TIME

READ : Esther 1:5-9
WRITE : Romans 12:2

. . . .

. . . .

REFLECT :
- Imagine the indulgent scene painted in today's passage. Who were the people serving?
- Read Romans 12:1-3, Matthew 6:19-21. What is God showing you?
- Contrast today's passage with Paul's words in Philippians 4:8-20 and Luke 14:7-11.
- Read *https://www.gotquestions.org/treasures-in-heaven.html* to see how you can store treasure in Heaven.
- Ask yourself the questions in today's quote and journal through your answers.

RESPOND :

. . . .

. . . .

. . . .

. . . .

PLAN TIME

THINGS TO DO (3-5 MAX) :

KEY EVENTS TODAY :

MOVE TIME

MORNING WATER ☐

B : _____

L : _____

D : _____

SNACK :

SIMPLE WORKOUT ☐

I WAS FIVE YEARS OLD WHEN I PRENTENDED TO BE A PIRATE. I just needed an eye patch to look the part. So, I quickly came up with a plan while gazing in the mirror. The gum I was chewing would make a perfect patch! Later, as my parents were removing pink, sticky bubble gum from my eyelashes and eyebrow, I learned this life truth: one bad decision can easily create a mess.

The bad decisions we read about in today's passage aren't humorous like my pirate story. But similarly, they do create a mess. Yet, they serve a purpose. They set the stage for God to reveal more of His providence enacted later in the Book of Esther.

We find Xerxes on the last day of the feast we discussed yesterday, feeling the effects of wine. God's Word doesn't specifically say he was drunk, but it would be no surprise if he was, since in Persian culture, it was acceptable. Herodotus (a Greek historian who lived in Persia during the time) reports that this was when decisions were made by the Persians, and the effects were cleaned up afterwards. It doesn't sound like a good time to be making any important decisions, does it?

He commands Vashti, his queen, to come display her beauty before the princes and other men. While nothing in the Bible, nor in early Jewish midrash points to Vashti being asked to go nude, later midrash does. Regardless, being asked to parade before drunken men was humiliating at best and was lewd and unsafe at worst. Herodotus reports that even to be looked at in public was beneath a queen. While Xerxes' request was out of custom, it fits with his personality! The proud, vain man wanted to display his trophy wife.

We'll never know why exactly Vashti refused Xerxes. I'd like to think she was refusing due to convictions. Babylonian rabbis, however, painted her as an anti-Semitic adulteress who didn't appear only because of an outbreak on her skin. Later rabbis wrote of her being a dignified woman who wouldn't stoop to her husband's request. The Bible doesn't tell us her motives, which I believe serves as a reminder not to assume things about others.

Regardless of Vashti's motives, her story can encourage us to stand up for our beliefs. And Xerxes' bad decision reminds us to think through things and seek godly counsel. God is always there to guide us and help us do the right thing (Psalm 32:8). All we have to do is ask!

— KEY VERSE —

On the seventh day, when the heart of the king was merry with wine, he commanded... to bring Queen Vashti before the king with her royal crown, in order to show the peoples and the princes her beauty, for she was lovely to look at. (Esther 1:10a-11)

Hello mornings
God. Plan. Move.

READ : Esther 1:10-15
WRITE : Esther 1:10a-11

. . . .

REFLECT :
- Read the passage again, noting the action words. Retell the story in your own words.
- What was the "mess" that Xerxes' request made? Vashti's refusal?
- How does the story in Acts 4:13-31 encourage you to stand firm in your beliefs?
- Do you need God's help and guidance? See John 14:26, Isaiah 58:11, James 1:5-6
- Spend time praising God for sending the Spirit that guides you. How is your life different because of His help?

RESPOND :

. . . .

THINGS TO DO (3-5 MAX) :

KEY EVENTS TODAY :

MORNING WATER ☐

B : _____
L : _____
D : _____

SNACK :

SIMPLE WORKOUT ☐

WEEK 2, DAY 1: ESTHER 1:16-22

I GRAB MY IPHONE AND SCAN THE HEADLINES. Clickbait titles try to persuade me to give precious minutes to petty tidbits. *"Selena Gomez Dons Eyebrow-raising T-shirt After Ex Justin Bieber Announces Engagement to Hailey Baldwin." "Emmy Nominations: All the Biggest Snubs and Surprises" "Museums and Films Planned for Thai Cave Where Soccer Team Was Rescued." "Camera Catches Mailman Stealing Family's Tomatoes."* People love to talk. The news articles and the tabloids are full of the world's gossip, largely made up of celebrities' lives.

The drama of Queen Vashti's autonomy? Oh, yeah. It was headline-worthy. We don't know if Queen Vashti influenced others because of her character or merely due to the influential position she held. Either way, the noblemen were all in an uproar over her refusal to come at King Xerxes' command to be an ornament of "show-and-tell." They feared her decision would send an unwelcome ripple effect throughout the kingdom, influencing wives of all levels to disrespect their husbands. Therefore Memucan, one of the king's noble advisors, judged Queen Vashti's actions and suggested a swift punishment to prevent the looming pandemonium of unruly wives in Persia.

From feasting to forsaken, famous Queen Vashti exits our story. An opening for queen of Persia is hot off the press, one designated for an influential woman. These events are really a part of a bigger narrative. God's hand of providence is moving to now allow Esther—an unlikely candidate being a Jewish adoptee—to be brought into the palace.

We all have influence and are influenced by others. 1 Corinthians 15:33 says, *"Do not be deceived: 'Bad company ruins good morals.'"* But the first part of Proverbs 13:22 says, "Whoever walks with the wise becomes wise." No matter what people are doing around us, we need to be careful that their lives aren't influencing us away from a biblical worldview. At the same time, we have the potential to be salt and light so others can be drawn to the Jesus in us. When you're wondering why you are in a peculiar circumstance, God might be placing you there on purpose.

— **KEY VERSE** —

For the queen's behavior will be made known to all women, causing them to look at their husbands with contempt, since they will say, "King Ahasuerus commanded Queen Vashti to be brought before him, and she did not come." (Esther 1:17)

READ : Esther 1:16-22
WRITE : Esther 1:17

. . . .

. . . .

REFLECT :
- Reread today's verses. Notice how influence played a role in the events.
- Check the following link to see the vast area that Vashti's influence could have spread:
  https://www.blueletterbible.org/images/TheGraphicBible/imageDisplay/tgb_074ab
- Pray and ask God to remove ungodly influences in your life and add godly influences.
- Look up Proverbs 10:19. Why do you think talking so much leads to sin?
- Who in your life do you have the potential to influence for God's glory?

RESPOND :

. . . .

. . . .

. . . .

. . . .

. . . .

. . . .

PLAN TIME

THINGS TO DO (3-5 MAX) :

KEY EVENTS TODAY :

MOVE TIME

MORNING WATER ☐

B : _____
L : _____
D : _____

SNACK :

SIMPLE WORKOUT ☐

MY FRIEND KIM'S TESTIMONY IS AMAZING. Abandoned at birth, her adoptive parents took her—and did her wrong. She was abused as a child in numerous ways and hated life. Then as a young adult, she found Jesus and discovered a God who would never abandon or abuse her. Now she's a seasoned speaker, minister, mother, and her followers often beg her to write a book because of the wisdom that pours from her mouth. But she wouldn't have gone from a horrific past to thriving in life if it weren't for the godly mentors that took the time to invest in her.

Mordecai's ancestor Kish was one of the captives carried away from Jerusalem. This meant that Mordecai was living in a "strange" land. Yet his faith in God was strong. Esther, adopted by her cousin Mordecai, was blessed to have his godly example and this influenced her character.

"One who refuses to seek the advice of others will eventually be led to a path of ruin. A mentor helps you to perceive your own weaknesses and confront them with courage. The bond between mentor and protege enables us to stay true to our chosen path until the very end."—Anonymous

Circumstances will be thrust in your lap, and you'll need to pull from your mentor's godly insight and previous training to help you through it. Esther's future, fated by an officer collecting her to be brought to the king's palace, meant she'd better respond with wisdom if it were to be at all pleasant. Evidently she did, because the first event we discover of the virgin captive is that she pleased Hegai, the king's eunuch, and won his favor.

Look at all the benefits she received from this (verse 9). How do we obtain favor? It comes from God. *"When a man's ways please the LORD, he makes even his enemies to be at peace with him"* (Proverbs 16:7).

Esther followed God, as we will see in the coming weeks, and had His favor. She was teachable, submissive, and obedient. When Mordecai commanded her not to reveal her Jewish roots, she yielded to his wise counsel. Even when Esther was under the palace roof, Mordecai continued to look after her welfare. Mentoring someone is an investment made in the kingdom of God; the return is God's glory.

— KEY VERSE —

Esther had not made known her people or kindred, for Mordecai had commanded her not to make it known. (Esther 2:10)

Hello mornings

God. Plan. Move.

READ : Esther 2:1-11
WRITE : Esther 2:10

REFLECT :
- Research others in the Bible who were adopted.
- Memorize the key verse.
- Research mentor/mentee pairs in the Bible. Here are a couple to get you started: Jethro/Moses Exodus 18, Moses/Joshua Joshua 4:14.
- Mentoring someone begins with being mentored. Who is mentoring you?
- Look up Proverbs 13:14 and 27:17. Ponder how they apply to mentorship.

RESPOND :

PLAN TIME

THINGS TO DO (3-5 MAX) :

KEY EVENTS TODAY :

MOVE TIME

MORNING WATER ☐

B : _____
L : _____
D : _____

SNACK :

SIMPLE WORKOUT ☐

WEEK 2, DAY 3: ESTHER 2:12-18

MY COUSINS WERE ALREADY BEAUTIFUL to my eight-year-old envious eyes. They seemed even more sparkly after they told me they had started modeling school to enter beauty pageants. I also wanted this, but my mom said no. Soon after, I landed the lead in the church musical. I was enraptured with the beauty preparations for the first night's performance. I got to wear makeup! All trepidation faded as the audience's applause wrapped my heart in glory. After the show, a man from the audience gave me several quarters. How thrilled I was with the attention! My parents talked me off a throne of glory afterwards, but the seed of pride lay planted nevertheless.

Esther, in the prime of her life, was whisked to the king's palace as one of the many young beautiful virgins who were candidates to be queen. A beauty pageant indeed. Adopted Esther was being purified along with all the other virgins, two six-month sessions of beautifying. A twelve-month wait also ensured the women weren't with child, claiming the king fathered a child that wasn't his. What really mattered was that the lady who would become queen would win the favor of the king. And Esther did: *"...the king loved Esther more than all the women, and she won grace and favor in his sight more than all the virgins"* (verse 17).

It seemed that it wasn't outward beauty alone that hooked his heart. Her character blossomed and bore beautiful fruit from the seeds planted by the mentoring in her earlier years. Her winning reputation was evident in verse 15, *"Esther was winning favor in the eyes of all who saw her."*

As a young Christian, we don't yet have the full revelation that God intends us to mature spiritually as we continue in our walk with Him. After we come into His kingdom, there is a period of purification—sanctification—where *"we are being transformed into the same image from one degree of glory to another"* (2 Corinthians 3:18). This is where God is working on our character and getting us ready as the Bride of Christ. One day we will see our King face-to-face. Now is the time to get ready.

— KEY VERSE —

Now when the turn came for each young woman to go in to King Ahasuerus, after being twelve months under the regulations for the women, since this was the regular period of their beautifying, six months with oil of myrrh and six months with spices and ointments for women... (Esther 2:12)

Hello mornings

God. Plan. Move.

READ : Esther 2:12-18
WRITE : Esther 2:12

....

....

....

REFLECT :
- Flip back to the reading from Week One, Day Three, and compare it to today's reading. How long was it before Queen Vashti left and Esther was brought in to King Ahasuerus?
- Look up 1 Thessalonians 5:23. What part of us does God wish to sanctify?
- Pray and ask God if there's a part of your heart He would like to sanctify.
- Illustrate or outline today's reading.
- Research more details about the virgins' purification process to see why it was necessary.

RESPOND :

....

....

....

....

....

....

PLAN TIME

THINGS TO DO (3-5 MAX) :

KEY EVENTS TODAY :

MOVE TIME

MORNING WATER ☐

B : _____

L : _____

D : _____

SNACK :

SIMPLE WORKOUT ☐

WEEK 2, DAY 4: ESTHER 2:19-23

WHEN I WAS A TEEN, I was the passenger sitting behind the driver in a van full of church attendees returning home from a service. The man driving and his co-pilot were in leadership in our church. I was keeping myself busy on the long ride back with books and a journal, but their conversation caught my ears. Being a pastor's kid, their obvious disagreement to how my parents ran the church concerned me. I was much too spiritually immature to understand the great majority of their conversation, but their pact to "never let it happen again" rings in my ears to this day. A few days later, these men took over the pulpit while my parents were out of town, and their verbal attack on my parents caused a church split. I wished many times over that I had understood so I could have warned my parents.

In today's reading, Mordecai was in the right place at the right time. Sitting at the king's gate provided him a more influential position, which gave him the opportunity to be like a watchman for the authority of the land. He overheard the eunuchs Bigthan and Teresh plotting to murder the king. We don't know the details of their reasons, but their conspiracy was born out of anger. In verse 21, we see that these eunuchs were supposed to be guarding the door in honor to the king. Ponder the irony.

Mordecai's wise response in revealing their sinister plot to Esther seemed to be divine providence in saving the king's life. Esther relayed Mordecai's urgent message to the king. After the investigation proved the two eunuchs were guilty of treason, they were hanged. *"...And it was recorded in the book of the chronicles in the presence of the king"* (verse 23), which later proved to be another move in the domino line of God's sovereign hand.

Mordecai knew the righteous response would be to try to save the king's life. He honored the king by his actions. This reminds me of Peter's instructions to *"Honor all people, love the brotherhood, fear God, honor the king"* (1 Peter 2:17, NASB). If you're ever in a precarious situation, honor others, especially ones who are in authority. God may be using you to fulfill His divine plam.

— KEY VERSE —

And this came to the knowledge of Mordecai, and he told it to Queen Esther, and Esther told the king in the name of Mordecai. (Esther 2:22)

Hello mornings

God. Plan. Move.

READ : Esther 2:19-23
WRITE : Esther 2:22

. . . .

. . . .

REFLECT :
- Write a paraphrase of today's reading in your journal.
- Read Romans 12:10. How does it say we should honor others?
- Check out Psalm 69:28; Luke 10:20; Revelation 3:5. What does the Bible say about God recording in books?
- Pray and ask God to show you how you can honor others in your daily life.
- Pray for those in authority over you.

RESPOND :

. . . .

. . . .

. . . .

. . . .

PLAN TIME

THINGS TO DO (3-5 MAX) :

KEY EVENTS TODAY :

MOVE TIME

MORNING WATER ☐

B : _____

L : _____

D : _____

SNACK :

SIMPLE WORKOUT ☐

WEEK 2, DAY 5: ESTHER 3:1-6

MY FRIENDS, FAMILY, AND FOES FAIL TO UNDERSTAND my firm commitment to obey God no matter the consequences. The same is the case in today's reading. We have scant facts without knowing Mordecai's motives in this pivotal point in Esther's drama. The king elevates Haman—said by some biblical scholars to be a descendant of the Amalekites, enemies of the Jews—to the highest place in the court. Packaged in his promotion is a direct command given by the king for his remaining servants to bow and worship this Haman. Mordecai, standing upright, conspicuous to all except the Persian monarch himself, leaves us grappling with a sufficient reason for his civil disobedience.

The only reason he gives when his fellow court minions sought an explanation day after day, is that he is a Jew. In other places in the Bible, Jews prostrated themselves before kings in a sign of respect (Genesis 33:3, 43:26; 1 Kings 1:16). So why didn't he bow? Various theories exist.

One, described by Rev. Joseph Benson, *"The kings of Persia, we know, required a kind of divine adoration from all who approached them; and, as they arrogated this to themselves, so they sometimes imparted it to their chief friends and favourites, which seems to have been the case with regard to Haman at this time."* If that were the case, his refusal is duly justified in keeping his heart pure from giving mere man divine honor.

Another stems from the apocryphal additions of Esther, a prayer by Mordecai, *"… you know, O Lord, that it was not in insolence or pride or for any love of glory that I did this, and refused to bow down to this proud Haman;…But I did this so that I might not set human glory above the glory of God, and I will not bow down to anyone but you, who are my Lord…"* (Greek Esther, Addition C; 13:12-14, NRSV).

The Jewish-Amalekite feud continues, yet another theory on the table. Whatever his reason, Mordecai felt it necessary to stand his ground despite the severe implications rendered. Upon discovering Mordecai's refusal, Haman's wrathful backlash is a malevolent agenda to destroy the entire Jewish community within the walls of the Persian Empire.

The ungodly won't understand our choice to obey God because the things of God are spiritually discerned (1 Corinthians 2:14).

— **KEY VERSE** —

Then the king's servants who were at the king's gate said to Mordecai, "Why do you transgress the king's command?" (Esther 3:3)

Hello mornings

God. Plan. Move.

READ : Esther 3:1-6
WRITE : Esther 3:3

....

....

REFLECT :
- Write down questions you have about today's passage. You can answer them later.
- Notice in our key verse how others observed Mordecai's life.
- Read more about the Jewish-Amalekite feud in Exodus 17:8-16.
- Research who God requires us to obey and the exception to the rule. Start in Hebrews 13, then Acts 5:29.
- Pray and ask God to reveal any area of your life where you aren't walking in obedience.

RESPOND :

....

....

....

....

PLAN TIME

THINGS TO DO (3-5 MAX) :

MOVE TIME

MORNING WATER ☐

B : _____

L : _____

D : _____

KEY EVENTS TODAY :

SNACK :

SIMPLE WORKOUT ☐

WEEK 3, DAY 1: ESTHER 3:7-11

REMEMBER MAGIC 8 BALLS? You ask a question, shake the ball, turn it over, and a generic answer appears. How about plucking the petals off a flower to determine if "he loves me, he loves me not"? Or the classic Rock Paper Scissors, or flipping a coin? These and many other games of chance were the decision makers of my childhood. My friends and I used them to determine everything from what we were going to play next, to whom we were going to marry and where we were going to live.

Human beings have been casting the lot in one form or another for as long as we've been on this earth. The Lord gave the Israelites the Urim and Thummin to help them determine His will (Exodus 28:30). It's troubling to face the unknown. Casting lots is an outward expression of seeking answers, a way to remove human bias from the decision.

Haman was no exception. *"In resorting to this method of ascertaining the most auspicious day for putting his atrocious scheme into execution, Haman acted as the kings and nobles of Persia have always done, never engaging in any enterprise without consulting the astrologers, and being satisfied as to the lucky hour."*—Jamieson, Fausset, and Brown

When Haman presented his plan to the king, he carefully worded his proposal, packing it with half-truths. There was a certain people scattered and dispersed among the kingdom. In fact, there were many. The Jewish people followed different laws and kept their religious traditions, even more so since many of the Jews had been allowed to return to Jerusalem and rebuild the temple. Finally, he threw in a promise for a good bit of money to make it all more appealing.

Ironically, though Haman was doing everything he could to ensure fate would be on his side, it was Mordecai, Esther, and his intended victims who ultimately benefited from his selection. The chosen date was eleven months away giving them ample time to deal with the impending massacre. It's one of those coincidences that pop up in this story that really isn't a coincidence at all. It is the providential hand of the Lord protecting his people.

—  KEY VERSE —

The lot is cast into the lap, but its every decision is from the LORD. (Proverbs 16:33)

Hello mornings

God. Plan. Move.

GOD TIME

READ : Esther 3:7-11
WRITE : Proverbs 16:33

REFLECT :
  – Research Biblical examples of "casting lots." Why is it no longer a practice today?
  – Read Psalm 2 and pray verses 10-12 over your civic leaders today.
  – Why do you suppose Haman targeted the whole nation instead of just Mordecai?
  – How do you know if a decision you make is "right" or "wrong"? Do you look for external "signs"? If so, what do you look for?
  – Read this article on discerning God's will: *https://bible.org/article/discerning-will-god*.

RESPOND :

PLAN TIME

THINGS TO DO (3-5 MAX) :

KEY EVENTS TODAY :

MOVE TIME

MORNING WATER ☐

B : _____
L : _____
D : _____

SNACK :

SIMPLE WORKOUT ☐

I AM A PART OF THE NAMELESS GENERATION between Gen X and Millenials. The chief characteristic of those born between the late 1970's and early 1980's is that we identify with aspects of both analogs—phones, answering machines, floppy disks, personal desktop computers—and digital technology—cell phones, streaming internet, laptops, tablets, and all that jazz. We are accustomed to the immediacy of texting, but we also remember the days of dial-up when communication was less immediate. Once upon a time, people had to wait for the morning or evening news to find out what was happening in the world. Today, news is so current, the story is breaking before it's finished happening! This leads to incomplete, sometimes entirely false information causing mass confusion and outrage.

Confusion might be our default setting, but the citizens of Susa were used to believing whatever the messengers of the king had to say. It might take a little more time to spread the word, but they could at least trust that what they were hearing was true. So when Haman's carefully plotted edict came out with instructions *"to destroy, to kill, and to annihilate all Jews, young and old, women and children, in one day"* the people were thrown into confusion (verse 13). It had to be true, but how could it be?

The Jewish people in this time and place had been born here. Perhaps their parents or grandparents had been offered the chance to return to Jerusalem, but they'd chosen to stay. They were comfortable, thriving, productive members of society. In an empire as large and tolerant as Persia, it's not hard to imagine the shock rippling throughout the city as they are told to prepare for the day when they must execute and plunder their neighbors. Haman had poisoned the well against this "certain people" to the king, but he made no such effort to badmouth them to the rest of the citizens (Esther 3:8). He didn't need to. The king's signet ring made the proclamation impossible not to obey. Was Haman worried at all about retaliation? It doesn't appear so.

It might not seem like a big deal on the surface, but suppose for a moment that the people of Susa hated their Jewish neighbors. What if they were hungry for their destruction? Would they have been able to wait almost a year for the king's permission to plunder and annihilate? Maybe this is another example of God's hand working in the background, ensuring that everything came to pass exactly as it needed to.

— **KEY VERSE** —

The couriers went out hurriedly by order of the king, and the decree was issued in Susa the citadel. And the king and Haman sat down to drink, but the city of Susa was thrown into confusion. (Esther 3:15)

Hello mornings

God. Plan. Move.

READ : Esther 3:12-15
WRITE : Esther 3:15

REFLECT :
- Where do you get your news today? What sources do you trust and why?
- Research the life of Jewish exiles. What benefits came out of that period of Israel's history?
- Why do you think King Ahasuerus approved Haman's plot?
- Look up Romans 13:1, Jeremiah 29:7, 1 Timothy 2:1-2, and 1 Peter 2:17. How are we to respond to our leaders? Are there exceptions? Check out Acts 5:29.
- What can we learn about taking advice from King Ahasuerus and Haman?

RESPOND :

PLAN TIME

THINGS TO DO (3-5 MAX) :

KEY EVENTS TODAY :

MOVE TIME

MORNING WATER ☐

B : _____
L : _____
D : _____

SNACK :

SIMPLE WORKOUT ☐

WEEK 3, DAY 3: ESTHER 4:1-5

SEPTEMBER 11, 2001. I remember exactly where I was when the news came that the World Trade Center Towers in New York City had each been hit by an airplane in an act of terrorism. I was a sophomore in college. I heard about it first from my British Literature teacher. After class, I went back to my dorm where my suitemates had the news playing. We watched. We hugged each other. We cried. I called my dad, scared and uncertain. He reminded me that God was still in control. Over the years, I have asked my peers what they were doing on that day, and everyone can recall where they were. Our shared grief bonded the nation together.

The Jewish citizens of Susa went into mourning as news of Haman's plot spread. They tore their clothes, sat in sackcloth and ashes, wept and wailed; all very physical signs of their deep distress. This generation had grown up in the Persian Empire. Life in Susa was all they'd ever known. They weren't treated like outcasts or looked on as slaves like in Egypt. They were comfortable, going about their business. Their time as exiles had served to sharpen the Jewish identity as God's people, a distinction that went beyond political borders. The temple in Jerusalem was rebuilt, the nation was rebuilding, and the people in Susa were keeping their traditions alive while also enjoying the acceptance of their neighbors and the prosperity of a well-established empire.

Esther was sheltered in her corner of the palace. There was no reason for the edict to be sent to her, so she was blissfully unaware of the trouble facing her people. Her Jewish heritage was unknown. When word of her cousin's very public display of mourning reached her ears, she chose to reach out in compassion. This is the first moment we see that Esther is more than just a pretty face. She certainly could have remained ignorant of the world outside, but her character wouldn't allow it.

Lawrence O. Richards writes in the *Illustrated Bible Handbook, "Providence does not mean that God violates any individual's freedom of choice. Each person in the Esther story acts in harmony with his own character, values, and beliefs, without any divine coercion."* Esther wasn't affected by the events in the city, but in reaching out, she demonstrates that she is willing to stand by her people in their time of grief. It's a precursor to the time when she would be needed to stand up for them.

— KEY VERSE —

And in every province, wherever the king's command and his decree reached, there was great mourning among the Jews, with fasting and weeping and lamenting, and many of them lay in sackcloth and ashes. When Esther's young women and her eunuchs came and told her, the queen was deeply distressed. (Esther 4:3-4a)

Hello mornings

God. Plan. Move.

READ : Esther 4:1-5
WRITE : Esther 4:3-4a

. . . .

. . . .

REFLECT :
- How does each person in the story act "in harmony with his own character, values, and beliefs"?
- Research Old Testament practices of mourning, tearing clothes, sackcloth, and ashes.
- How do you respond to sorrow and grief in your own life?
- Make a list of things you can do to show compassion for someone suffering.
- How do you think you would respond if you were one of the Jews in Susa?

RESPOND :

. . . .

. . . .

. . . .

. . . .

. . . .

PLAN TIME

THINGS TO DO (3-5 MAX) :

KEY EVENTS TODAY :

MOVE TIME

MORNING WATER ☐

B : _____
L : _____
D : _____

SNACK :

SIMPLE WORKOUT ☐

IS THERE ANYTHING MORE FRUSTRATING THAN FACING INJUSTICE and knowing you are powerless to stop it? I've always wanted to be in a position of authority. Not because I'm power hungry, but because I want to affect real change. I once worked as the Human Resources Associate in a small company. Everything related to employee relations fell under my administration, from performance reviews to employee benefits. While I had plenty of discretion in my day-to-day work, I had no actual power to make any policy changes. I could take my ideas to my boss, but unless he decided it was worth pursuing (and he wasn't a big fan of any kind of change), the dream died there. It was frustrating to see things that could be improved and to have my hands tied. It was difficult to be on the frontlines, face-to-face with the people who were affected by the poorly written policy or dealing with untrained management and be powerless to give anything but a sympathetic ear. I desperately wanted to make a difference for them but simply was not in a position to do so.

Esther must have felt something like this when she learned of the trouble facing her people. Mordecai, because of his position in court, had a copy of the document and was able to share all the details, including the money Haman planned to exchange. Esther might have been isolated, but she was smart, and the scope of the problem was not lost on her.

As queen, Esther was in a position of influence but not, at the moment, favor. Queens in this time and place were little more than ornamental. They had a responsibility to provide as many children as possible to ensure the stability of the king's line. They lived in separate apartments within the palace, closely guarded, ready at the king's pleasure.

*"Her case was at present very discouraging. Providence so ordered it that, just at this juncture, she was under a cloud, and the king's affections cooled towards her, for she had been kept from his presence thirty days, that her faith and courage might be the more tried, and **that God's goodness** in the favour she now found with the king notwithstanding **might shine the brighter**."*—Matthew Henry, emphasis added

What could she possibly offer her people from this position? Anything she could do would require a great dependence on God's intervention.

— KEY VERSE —

All the king's servants and the people of the king's provinces know that if any man or woman goes to the king inside the inner court without being called, there is but one law—to be put to death, except the one to whom the king holds out the golden scepter so that he may live. But as for me, I have not been called to come in to the king these thirty days. (Esther 4:11)

Hello mornings
God. Plan. Move.

GOD TIME

READ : Esther 4:6-11
WRITE : Esther 4:11

REFLECT :
- Read Ecclesiastes 3:16. What injustices in the world are heavy on your heart?
- Write out Ecclesiastes 3:17.
- Have you ever faced a situation where you felt helpless? How did you respond?
- In 2 Corinthians 12:9, Paul says, *"...I will boast all the more gladly of my weaknesses, so that the power of Christ may rest upon me."* How does this apply to Esther's position?
- Why did Mordecai command Esther to go before the king (verse 8) instead of going himself?

RESPOND :

PLAN TIME

THINGS TO DO (3-5 MAX) :

KEY EVENTS TODAY :

MOVE TIME

MORNING WATER ☐

B : _____
L : _____
D : _____

SNACK :

SIMPLE WORKOUT ☐

WEEK 3, DAY 5: ESTHER 4:12-17

I HAVE A SECRET DESIRE TO WRITE A NOVEL. I've been a writer my whole life, but I've never finished a novel. I've started a million stories and filled notebooks with character sketches, plot points, and notes on everything from fairy legends to story "how to" guides.

One thing I have learned is that there are two crucial elements in every great story and they are often mistaken as being the same thing: the inciting incident and the key event. The inciting incident is the thing that starts the story. If you were to summarize the book in a sentence or two, this is what the story is about. The key event, on the other hand, is the moment the protagonist engages in the action. The point of no return. The story and the character are forever altered from this point forward.

I've gone back and forth in my mind about what the inciting incident and key event are in the book of Esther. Keeping in mind that the book is an ancient Hebrew writing about real people and events, the author probably wasn't following the rules of modern novel structure. The whole book stacks up so neatly towards the climax, that it's difficult to pinpoint these two pivotal moments.

Like dominos, each moment of the story leads to the next. The King orders Vashti to appear at the banquet. Clink. Vashti refuses. Clink. The king banishes Vashti. Clink. A contest is declared. Clink. Esther is chosen. Clink. The dominos fall as the story goes on.

But now we come to the heart of the story: Haman's plot to exterminate the Jewish people has set things in motion. Inciting incident. Esther has reached out to Mordecai and now has a full picture of the trouble facing her people. Mordecai tells her that she will not escape their fate, but who's to say? A docile, obedient queen whose heritage is unknown might escape notice. As Mordecai points out in verse 14, she can choose to stay silent, and help will come from another place. God will not abandon His people, even if Esther does.

That's what makes this moment key. Esther chooses to act on behalf of her people. Regardless of the personal consequences, she allows God to use her for such a time as this. I love that she doesn't cast a lot but calls for a fast, further demonstrating that the God who has divinely guided her life thus far will continue to do so.

— KEY VERSE —

Go, gather all the Jews to be found in Susa, and hold a fast on my behalf, and do not eat or drink for three days, night or day. I and my young women will also fast as you do. Then I will go to the king, though it is against the law, and if I perish, I perish. (Esther 4:16)

Hello mornings
God. Plan. Move.

GOD TIME

READ : Esther 4;12-17
WRITE : Esther 4:16

....

....

REFLECT :
- Review the events leading up to Esther's decision. How does each one affect the next?
- Esther chooses to participate in God's plan, recognizing that it may cost her. How willing are you to follow God when things are difficult or risky?
- What moments in your life could be defined as "key events"?
- What other methods of salvation could the Jewish people have considered?
- Research the practice of fasting. Why did Esther ask for her people to fast?

RESPOND :

....

....

....

....

....

....

....

....

PLAN TIME

THINGS TO DO (3-5 MAX) :

KEY EVENTS TODAY :

MOVE TIME

MORNING WATER ☐

B : _____

L : _____

D : _____

SNACK :

SIMPLE WORKOUT ☐

WEEK 4, DAY 1: ESTHER 5:1-8

FAMILY NIGHT WAS UPON US AGAIN. Our daughter set the theme: royals. Out came the china and the dress-up clothes. Bending to the wishes of my children, I tried on banquet dresses leftover from high school. I'll admit, donning my prom dress (at age 35) felt pretty good. Slipping into a gown designed for a grand affair had me standing a little straighter, sitting a bit taller, chin lifted ever-so-slightly. An air of confidence accompanied me throughout our mannerly dinner and timer-guided portraits. But, before dinner, when I put on oven mitts to pull out our meal, I chuckled at the paradox, playing the role of cook and queen simultaneously. And yet, isn't that how life often is?

Life provides opportunities for tasks both glorious and mundane. In John 13, Jesus demonstrated this paradox by taking up the servant task of washing His disciples' feet. There, the King of Kings bowed low, His confidence in who He was making holy a humble task. Esther, however, an orphaned Jew far from the homeland of her people certainly had little expectation for a future position of royalty. But, once chosen to be queen, royalty became her new reality. Today, we see that Esther *"put on her royal robes"* before going to face the king (Esther 5:1). She had already spent time in prayer and fasting; time with the Lord which certainly equipped Esther with confidence. The time had come to remember who she was: royal.

As we read in last week's passage, approaching the king without invitation placed one's life at the king's mercy, risking even death. When Esther prepared for this dangerous mission to petition the king, she dressed with confidence in her identity as queen and in her heritage as one of God's chosen people. Esther's confidence ultimately rested in knowing that God, in His providence, had positioned her to impact radical change and save many lives. This was an act of obedience, a step of boldness. God surely guided the heart of the king to grant mercy and favor to Queen Esther in not only allowing her approach, but also by placing high priority upon quickly granting her request. By walking in obedience and confidence, submitted to the guiding hand of God, Esther tasted a great victory.

— **KEY VERSE** —

And when the king saw Queen Esther standing in the court, she won favor in his sight, and he held out to Esther the golden scepter that was in his hand... (Esther 5:2a)

Hello mornings

God. Plan. Move.

READ : Esther 5:1-8
WRITE : Esther 5:2a

. . . .

. . . .

REFLECT :
  – Read Hebrews 10:39. How does this relate to today's passage?
  – Read Isaiah 62:2-4. Ask the Lord: How do you see me?
  – How would today be different if you approached it from confidence in your royal identity?
  – Journal: Is there an area of life God is asking you to step out in confident obedience?
  – How is the favor the king gave to Esther similar to God's favor on us? How is it different?

RESPOND :

. . . .

. . . .

. . . .

. . . .

PLAN TIME	MOVE TIME
THINGS TO DO (3-5 MAX) :	**MORNING WATER** ☐
	B : _____
	L : _____
	D : _____
KEY EVENTS TODAY :	**SNACK :**
	SIMPLE WORKOUT ☐

WEEK 4, DAY 2: ESTHER 5:9-14

AS A TEENAGER, my communication skills left something to be desired. Through a horrible miscommunication on my part, I deeply hurt someone I cared about, someone who cared deeply for me. In his pain, he and his friends turned that passion against me in hatred. Though I lived longing for people to like me, quite the people-pleaser, avoiding conflict of any kind, I found myself at the center of attack. While no physical harm came my way, they set out to make life miserable for me and make their hatred known.

Reading through our passage for today, I'm deeply moved by Mordecai's conviction and persistent commitment to obey the commandments of the Lord. By refusing to bow down, Mordecai asserted that he would never give divine honor, which belongs only to God, to a mere man. Have I ever been so bold? So unwilling to bend to another's plan for me that attempted to usurp the honor due only to God? While the attack on my character in that high school season emerged from my own inability to communicate clearly, Mordecai encountered a hatred so great that Haman planned in detail Mordecai's demise. The hatred Mordecai encountered, born from resentment, pointed directly to his identity as a Jew.

But, Mordecai had a choice to make, just as we do. He chose to remain at the king's gate. During biblical times, the gate often represented justice as people would argue their cases before the elders of the city. Mordecai, in remaining at the gate, was able to overhear and foil the plot against the king (Esther 2:21). He remained firm, expecting justice to prevail, knowing that true justice could only come from the Lord. Thank goodness for a God who makes things right, even if it's not in our timing or in a way we can grasp in the midst of the turmoil. At times, this "good" that God is working out on our behalf may be beyond our finite understanding. But, as our key verse today says, we can always trust that God is working all things for our ultimate good. Through discussion and forgiveness, my friend and I later reconciled. In Mordecai's case, God had already laid out a plan for his good, for his protection and promotion. As we'll read later this week, Haman's hatred would become his own demise.

— KEY VERSE —

And we know that for those who love God all things work together for good, for those who are called according to his purpose. (Romans 8:28)

Hello mornings

God. Plan. Move.

READ : Esther 5:9-14
WRITE : Romans 8:28

REFLECT :
- Ask Jesus to reveal how He was present and working in the midst of a conflict.
- Read Proverbs 19:23. How is victory through obedience seen in this verse?
- Hebrew understanding states the name "Haman" means "noise." How does this compare with the voice of God which is described as a "whisper"? (See 1 Kings 19:11-12)
- Memorize today's key verse.
- Consider: Do your closest friends encourage you towards obedience or bitterness?

RESPOND :

PLAN TIME

THINGS TO DO (3-5 MAX) :

KEY EVENTS TODAY :

MOVE TIME

MORNING WATER ☐

B : _____
L : _____
D : _____

SNACK :

SIMPLE WORKOUT ☐

WEEK 4, DAY 3: ESTHER 6:1-9

LOOKING INTO THE EYES OF MY HUSBAND AND CHILDREN, I imagine how things could have turned out much differently. When I was a child, my family lost our home. For five months, we lived with my grandparents nearby in Houston. Tensions eventually ran high as unknowns stacked. Another set of grandparents, living five hours away in the Dallas-Fort Worth metroplex, invited us to come stay with them while we got our feet back under us. Eight years later, I would meet my husband only a few miles away from that home. There, we would raise children, find our church home, and encounter God's truth for our freedom and identity. My family's eviction was the only reason I had come to the DFW area, making a new home. But God took what was intended for our harm and destruction and created something new and beautiful.

Although in the Book of Esther, God's name is never mentioned, we see His hand move powerfully. While Haman spent his evening planning Mordecai's demise, God caused the king's sleepless night to result in plans to honor Mordecai. Not only is honor rather than destruction being planned, but Haman will be the one to imagine the means and bestow it. Haman, the very man who intended to destroy Mordecai, will instead become God's conduit of blessing. Proverbs 21:1 says, *"The king's heart is a stream of water in the hand of the Lord; He turns it wherever He will."* Five years had passed since Mordecai saved the king's life. Why should the king decide the very night before Mordecai was to be hanged, unbeknownst to the king, that Mordecai must be honored for his deed? Coincidence?

Poring through the pages of Esther, and the entirety of the Bible, many stories seem to have a coincidental bent. Even as we consider our lives, we may flippantly give credit to coincidence. However, there truly is no coincidence: there is simply the reality of choice and God's ability to create opportunities. Through our choices, or even despite them, God is moving. Will we partner with Him in His movements? Will we have willing eyes to see Providence at hand?

— KEY VERSE —

So Haman came in, and the king said to him, "What should be done to the man whom the king delights to honor?" (Esther 6:6a)

Hello mornings
God. Plan. Move.

READ : Esther 6:1-9
WRITE : Esther 6:6a

. . . .

. . . .

REFLECT :
– In Esther 6:4, the king, seeking someone to partner with him in giving Mordecai honor, asks, "Who is in the court?" Consider: Are you in God's court, ready to partner with His purposes?
– When has a seemingly terrible circumstance turned out for your good?
– Meditate on Proverbs 21:1. Ask God to lead your heart.
– Read Acts 16:6-10. Invite the Lord to interrupt and share His heart with you.
– Ask the Lord: How are you moving in my circumstances today?

RESPOND :

. . . .

. . . .

. . . .

. . . .

PLAN TIME

THINGS TO DO (3-5 MAX) :

KEY EVENTS TODAY :

MOVE TIME

MORNING WATER ☐

B : _____
L : _____
D : _____

SNACK :

SIMPLE WORKOUT ☐

WEEK 4, DAY 4: ESTHER 6:10-14

TEACHING THE WORD OF GOD has become a great passion of mine. But it wasn't always so. Even the idea of stepping in front of a crowd to speak sent trembling through me, certainty that I would never, ever be a public speaker. But one day, through another Christian's encouragement, God revealed a piece of His purpose for my life: communicating through the spoken word. Because in the months leading up to that moment, I had been developing depth and trust in my relationship with Him, when I heard this word, I received it. I said, "Lord, I don't know how that will look, but if you want to work through me in that way, I'll trust you." In that instant, fear broke off of me. It would be years later when my first opportunity to speak would come, but I was ready with my "yes." Simply agreeing with what God said about me shifted the course of my life and derailed the enemy's plans to keep my mouth shut.

When Haman came to the king that fateful night, the plot to extinguish the Jews still existed. But, beyond that, Haman, out of his hateful bitterness and desire for exultation, had made specific plans of destruction against Mordecai. The only human Haman seemed willing to obey was the king. And the king had quite different plans for Mordecai. So, in a twist of providence, Haman, by obeying the king, spoke life and honor over Mordecai. Even though Haman's heart was to destroy Mordecai, his words pointed to the near future where the humble Mordecai would live a life greatly honored above all others in the kingdom.

We partner with God when we listen to Him, obey, and speak in agreement with what He says. God's words are infinitely more powerful than the circumstances surrounding us. Even when we don't see how His goodness could exist in such dire situations, we can speak His promises, trusting in who He is. Even when we don't "feel it" we can still "speak it" and therefore agree with the Lord's plans rather than the enemy's plans. Our agreement makes the world of difference. Will we agree with the life God speaks over us.

— KEY VERSE —

Haman took the robes and the horse, and he dressed Mordecai and led him through the square of the city, proclaiming before him, "Thus shall it be done to the man whom the king delights to honor." (Esther 6:11)

Hello mornings
God. Plan. Move.

READ : Esther 6:10-14
WRITE : Esther 6:11

REFLECT :
  – Meditate on and memorize Proverbs 18:21.
  – Pay close attention to your words today. Are they serving life or death?
  – What promise of God are you trusting Him for today? Thank Him now for the victory and life He has planned for you.
  – Ask the Lord: Is there something I'm afraid to do that you want to equip me for?
  – Read Romans 12:10. How can you give honor to those in your life today?

RESPOND :

PLAN TIME

THINGS TO DO (3-5 MAX) :

KEY EVENTS TODAY :

MOVE TIME

MORNING WATER ☐

B : _____
L : _____
D : _____

SNACK :

SIMPLE WORKOUT ☐

WHEN THE CALL CAME IN saying that my father-in-law had suffered a stroke, my husband and I were shocked. A die-hard Olympic fan, my husband's father had traveled to Vancouver to attend the games with a friend. One morning, my father-in-law began babbling incomprehensibly. Something clearly was wrong. Rushed to the hospital, far from home and family, things didn't look good. My husband, Steve, needed to get to Vancouver, but how? That season of life for us was incredibly tight financially; we had no way to afford traveling from our home in Texas to Vancouver. Remembering my grandparents' long careers with an airline, I gave them a call. They were all too happy to help, securing us a buddy pass so that Steve could fly to his dad's side. A week of traveling and hospitals ensued, thankfully ending with my father-in-law at home, alive and safe. Had we not had the favor of my grandparents' airline connection, I'm not sure what would have happened. Through no ability or resource of our own, fully reliant upon our association to another person, we experienced victory laid upon the foundation of favor.

Steps toward salvation came upon the Jews in a most unexpected way, as God placed Esther in a position of favor. Only the king had power to save the Jews Haman intended to destroy. And, knowing that she had found favor with the king, Esther reached out in boldness to request salvation for her people and denounce the plans of their enemy, Haman.

Esther's boldness, obedience, and reliance on the favor of the king are a type and shadow of Jesus' actions on our behalf. Jesus, aware of the schemes of Satan for our destruction, boldly lived, teaching the kingdom of God. He obeyed His Father, even to the point of a torturous death. And, He relied upon God's favor to save His people from demise through His once-for-all sacrifice. Favor laid the way for salvation to enter in, for life to defeat death. We have no ability or resource of our own that can save us from eternal separation from God. Our salvation, here in the present and throughout eternity, depends not on our personal goodness, but only on the favor we enjoy when we receive the sacrifice Jesus made in our place.

— KEY VERSE —

Then Queen Esther answered, "If I have found favor in your sight, O king, and if it please the king, let my life be granted me for my wish, and my people for my request." (Esther 7:3)

Hello mornings

God. Plan. Move.

READ : Esther 7:1-6
WRITE : Esther 7:3

....

....

REFLECT :
- When you received a gift that was beyond your means to gain on your own, how did you feel?
- Meditate on 1 Peter 2:9 and your declared, royal identity.
- Ask the Lord to make Jesus' sacrifice and your salvation new and real to you today.
- Spend time in prayer for the salvation of loved ones who don't yet know Jesus.
- Read Proverbs 8:35. Ask the Lord to help you better see His favor upon you today.

RESPOND :

....

....

....

....

....

....

PLAN TIME

THINGS TO DO (3-5 MAX) :

KEY EVENTS TODAY :

MOVE TIME

MORNING WATER ☐

B : _____

L : _____

D : _____

SNACK :

SIMPLE WORKOUT ☐

WEEK 5, DAY 1: ESTHER 7:7-10

"The Lord has made himself known; he has executed judgment; the wicked are snared in the work of their own hands." (Psalm 9:16)

IT CAN SEEM SO DIFFICULT TO HOLD OUR TONGUES sometimes when we feel the need to speak up and defend ourselves, rather than being patient, wise, or discerning. At my old job, there were a couple of people that I knew God had deliberately placed in my path for me to practice loving the unlovely. Of course, these people weren't wicked in the sense that Haman was, they were just unbelievers in positions of some influence with a penchant for thinking that they were always right. The temptation was often strong to get pulled into arguments that would lead nowhere or to say something sarcastic when attitudes were perceived as haughty.

Sometimes I chose to react, rather than giving those thoughts over to the Lord, following that selfish desire to say the first thing that popped into my head. When I did, I usually regretted it afterward. Esther, however, was wise and waited on Mordecai's godly counsel; she knew that she would only have one chance to get this right–one chance to say either the right thing that would save her and her people or the wrong thing that would condemn them all. She was able to do this because she trusted Mordecai, the one who had raised her, as her earthly protector and provider. Her trust in the Lord must have been deeper, though, to make a request such as she did of the most powerful man in the world. And her trust in God was rewarded as she saw Him humble Haman, orchestrating it so that he would be hung on the very gallows that he had ordered built for Mordecai.

Words are important. Our silences are important, too. When we rely on God's wisdom, we can build bridges, rather than burn them. We can make His name famous and spread the Gospel. We cannot control the outcome, and we may still be hurt in the end, but when our speech is led by the Spirit, then it will be fruitful according to His will. *"Death and life are in the power of the tongue, and those who love it will eat its fruits."* (Proverbs 18:21) Sometimes, God will use the fruit of our lips to bring about the justice we long for, as He did with Esther, while other times we might not see that justice this side of heaven. Either way, He *will* make Himself known.

— KEY VERSE —

So they hanged Haman on the gallows that he had prepared for Mordecai. Then the wrath of the king abated. (Esther 7:10)

Hello mornings
God. Plan. Move.

GOD TIME

READ : Esther 7:7-10
WRITE : Esther 7:10

REFLECT :
- Reread Esther 5:14. How do you see God's sovereignty in this verse after reading chapter 7?
- Read Psalm 94:23 and Proverbs 11:5-6. What do these verses imply about justice?
- Meditate on and memorize Proverbs 18:21.
- Write down some positive and negative examples of fruit produced by your own tongue recently.
- Pray for God to lead your tongue to bear life-giving fruit today.

RESPOND :

PLAN TIME

THINGS TO DO (3-5 MAX) :

KEY EVENTS TODAY :

MOVE TIME

MORNING WATER ☐

B : _____
L : _____
D : _____

SNACK :

SIMPLE WORKOUT ☐

MY ENGAGEMENT STORY IS SIMPLE. After being apart for nine weeks, my boyfriend made supper for us, and we went for a walk at twilight. I noticed that he seemed to get nervous when we approached a lighted, swinging bridge over the river. Suddenly, he got down on one knee and asked if we could spend the rest of our lives together and if I would be his wife. Eventually, I remembered to say "Yes," and 11 years of marriage and three kids later, I am still overwhelmingly glad that I did. To this day, my husband says that even though we had already talked about God's plan for marriage in our lives and he knew that I wanted to marry him, there was still that fear that something had changed my mind, that perhaps I had "come to my senses" and would shut him down with a "No."

I can comprehend what my husband went through as he worked up the nerve to ask what was probably the most important question of his life, and I can empathize. But Esther's situation is almost inconceivable when you consider the danger she put herself in by once again coming into the king's presence uncalled, as *"she fell at his feet and wept and pleaded."* (v. 3) Her submission to the king is a picture of Jesus' submission to the Father as He drew near to the cross, for we see both Esther and Jesus interceding for God's people.

*"Therefore he is the mediator of a new covenant, so that those who are called may receive the promised eternal inheritance, since a death has occurred that redeems them from the transgressions committed under the first covenant.... For Christ has entered, not into holy places made with hands, which are copies of the true things, but into heaven itself, now **to appear in the presence of God on our behalf.**"* (Hebrews 9:15, 24, emphasis added)

My husband regarded the reward of having me as his bride as greater than the risk of being rejected, just as Esther regarded the reward of the Jews' salvation as greater than the risk of her own death (Esther 4:16). Similarly, Jesus regarded the reward of the salvation of many and bringing glory to the Father as greater than the reproach of the cross. And just as I am thankful that God gave my husband the courage to ask the question he needed to, I am thankful for the courage He gave Esther that foreshadows the greater fortitude of our Savior at the cross.

— KEY VERSE —

Then Esther spoke again to the king. She fell at his feet and wept and pleaded with him to avert the evil plan of Haman the Agagite and the plot that he had devised against the Jews. (Esther 8:3)

Hello mornings

God. Plan. Move.

GOD TIME

READ : Esther 8:1-7
WRITE : Esther 8:3

. . . .

. . . .

REFLECT :
- Read John 11:31-33. How does Mary's posture toward Jesus mirror Esther's toward the king?
- What attitude does this posture communicate?
- Read Hebrews 9:15-28. We know Esther appeared twice before the king; how is Jesus' appearance before God different?
- Ask God to reveal areas in your life where He is asking you to submit to Him.
- Pray for the Lord's help to trust Him with the outcome as you submit to Him in this area.

RESPOND :

. . . .

. . . .

. . . .

. . . .

PLAN TIME

THINGS TO DO (3-5 MAX) :

KEY EVENTS TODAY :

MOVE TIME

MORNING WATER ☐

B : _____

L : _____

D : _____

SNACK :

SIMPLE WORKOUT ☐

WEEK 5, DAY 3: ESTHER 8:8-14

THIS PAST YEAR, I had the opportunity not only to study the Book of Romans but also to help teach it to a group of young toddlers. As we approached the middle of the book, we reminded the children of the truths that nothing stops God from loving us and that God is in charge. Explaining these huge, overarching themes of the Bible in terms that little hearts could understand helped my own heart to understand them in new ways.

I imagine that the children of Israel learned these lessons in new ways, too, as they watched God bring victory over Haman's proclamation and show His protection and care through Mordecai's proclamation, which would allow the Jews to defend themselves from their enemies and even plunder their goods. *"What then shall we say to these things? If God is for us, who can be against us? … Who shall separate us from the love of Christ? Shall tribulation, or distress, or persecution, or famine, or nakedness, or danger, or sword?"* (Romans 8:31, 35)

The Jews had the very real threat of any one of the troubles listed in Romans 8:35 hanging over their heads. Their concerns were real and prominent, but they had something that their enemies did not: a God who had chosen them and loved them. His sovereign control over the politics of a vast empire allowed Mordecai to write an edict in the king's name that would protect His people from the king's former edict (v. 8). And, as we will see over the next two days, God's love for the Jews was made evident as He brought more people to Himself and gave them victory over their enemies.

Yet in all these things we are more than conquerors and gain an overwhelming victory through Him who loved us [so much that He died for us]. For I am convinced …that neither death, nor life, nor angels, nor principalities, nor things present and threatening, nor things to come, nor powers, nor height, nor depth, nor any other created thing, will be able to separate us from the [unlimited] love of God, which is in Christ Jesus our Lord. (Romans 8:37-39, AMP)

If we allow God to fix our eyes on Jesus while in the midst of trials and tribulation, we will have opportunities to see God's sovereign power and experience His unlimited love for us. When we look at our troubles through the lens of who God is, we may not understand our circumstances, but we will understand *Him* more.

— KEY VERSE —

But you may write as you please with regard to the Jews, in the name of the king, and seal it with the king's ring, for an edict written in the name of the king and sealed with the king's ring cannot be revoked. (Esther 8:8)

Hello mornings

God. Plan. Move.

READ : Esther 8:8-14
WRITE : Esther 8:8

....

....

....

REFLECT :
- Look up Daniel 6:8. How were laws written in that time different than those written today?
- Look back at Esther 3:13 and compare it with 8:11. How did God provide for His people through Mordecai?
- Read Romans 8:31-39, and meditate on our security in God's love through Jesus Christ.
- How does Jesus' death grant us overwhelming victory?
- Pray that, when trials come, God will allow you to be convinced of His love for you.

RESPOND :

....

....

....

....

....

....

PLAN TIME

THINGS TO DO (3-5 MAX) :

KEY EVENTS TODAY :

MOVE TIME

MORNING WATER ☐

B : _____

L : _____

D : _____

SNACK :

SIMPLE WORKOUT ☐

WHEN WE FOUND OUT WE WERE PREGNANT AGAIN shortly after the miscarriage of our first child, I kept coming back to the truth that God has written out *"the days that were formed for me."* (Psalm 139:16) Every day each of our babies' hearts had or would beat was a gift from the Lord; yet, I still found myself arguing with my heavenly Father one Sunday morning at church. As I struggled to sing the words of the worship song projected on the screen, I realized, in that moment, I wanted to hold my child–alive and healthy–more than I wanted God's will for my life. In that moment, I clearly thought, "Lord, nothing you have for me could be better than having this baby be safe and healthy and with *me*."

Instantly, the Lord impressed upon my heart how untrue that statement was: *"Whom have I in heaven but you? And there is **nothing on earth that I desire besides you**. My flesh and my heart may fail, but God is the strength of my heart and my portion forever. … **But for me it is good to be near God;** I have made the Lord God my refuge, that I may tell of all your works."* (Psalm 73:25-26, 28, emphasis added) I knew then that if the Lord took my child, I would praise Him now and rejoice when we were reunited with Christ in heaven. In His gracious love, He led our now six-year-old son safely to our arms, and we are forever changed and forever grateful.

The Jews, who awhile ago were under a dark cloud, dejected and disgraced, now had light and gladness, joy and honour, a feast and a [holiday]. If they had not been threatened and in distress they would not have had occasion for this extraordinary joy. Thus are God's people sometimes made to sow in tears that they may reap in so much the more joy.—Matthew Henry

If the Jews had not experienced the threat of persecution and death, they would not have experienced God's salvation and display of sovereign power. If the natives around them had not seen God's people go from certain destruction to favor and power, then they would not have declared themselves Jews. With our limited knowledge, it can be difficult to understand why the Lord would have us *"walk through the valley of the shadow of death,"* but we would not otherwise know His comfort or see His goodness and mercy displayed so surely (Psalm 23:4).

— KEY VERSE —

… there was gladness and joy among the Jews, a feast and a holiday. And many from the peoples of the country declared themselves Jews, for fear of the Jews had fallen on them. (Esther 8:17b)

Hello mornings
God. Plan. Move.

GOD TIME

READ : Esther 8:15-17
WRITE : Esther 8:17b

....

....

REFLECT :
- How was Mordecai honored here, and how does this differ from the fate intended for him?
- How did the Jews respond to God's deliverance? How did the people of Susa respond?
- Read Psalm 107:13-15. What should be the response of God's people to His deliverance?
- In what ways can you give glory to God when He brings you through a hard situation?
- If you are walking through something difficult, pray that those around you would be impacted by your testimony.

RESPOND :

....

....

....

....

....

PLAN TIME

THINGS TO DO (3-5 MAX) :

KEY EVENTS TODAY :

MOVE TIME

MORNING WATER ☐

B : _____

L : _____

D : _____

SNACK :

SIMPLE WORKOUT ☐

WEEK 5, DAY 5: ESTHER 9:1-10

MY FRESHMAN YEAR OF COLLEGE, my new church was going through Rick Warren's book, *The Purpose Driven Life*. In the very first paragraph, I read these simple, yet life-changing words: "It's not about you." As I was embarking on this new adventure, the most important thing I needed to know was that I had been created as part of God's design to know Him and bring glory to Him. "You were born *by* his purpose and for his purpose. … Focusing on ourselves will never reveal our life's purpose."

The choices I would make in that first year of adulthood boiled down to whether I wanted to live for myself or live for the Lord. As I struggled through papers and tests, finances, and waking up early for church on Sundays when I had no roommate, I made decisions each day, each moment either to trust in myself or trust in the Lord. God was building in me a foundation of looking to Him first in the midst of doubt or trouble, teaching me to look at the bigger picture of His unfolding plan.

It can be difficult to read in this chapter about the deaths of so many and give glory to God. We need to step back, look at the whole picture, and remember that these men despised the Jews and fully intended to kill them. We should praise the Lord as we see His sovereign hand grant His people *"mastery over those who hated them"* and turn the government from persecuting the Jews to helping them. God's Word is full of His examples of orchestrating evil or seemingly impossible situations for good: Joseph saving thousands from famine after being persecuted by his own brothers (Genesis 50:20), Daniel's rescue from the lion's den that led the king to worship God (Daniel 6), a pagan widow becoming an ancestor of Jesus (Ruth 4), and enemies of God brought from darkness and death into light and life through the cross of Christ (Romans 5).

"If you would truly know what's done
Upon the earth, you have to ask: / What power is hid behind the mask
Of man's design? Am I the queen / Because of looks? What does it mean
That Haman hung on gallows made / For Mordecai, and that the blade
Aimed at the Jews, instead of these / Was thrust against their enemies?"—John Piper

God is indeed sovereign. And He is always, always good. Even if we cannot see the good, we can still look to the One who is Faithful and True (Revelation 19:11).

— **KEY VERSE** —

… On the very day when the enemies of the Jews hoped to gain the mastery over them, the reverse occurred: the Jews gained mastery over those who hated them. (Esther 9:1b)

Hello mornings
God. Plan. Move.

GOD TIME

READ : Esther 9:1-10
WRITE : Esther 9:1b

. . . .

. . . .

REFLECT :
- Study Romans 5:12-21. How did Jesus accomplish the reverse of what occurred through Adam?
- Read Romans 5:8-11 and praise God for His reconciliation through Jesus Christ.
- Jot down any other biblical examples you can think of where God worked out evil for good.
- Look up Revelation 21:3-6. What is the ultimate good God has in store for us?
- Pray that God would enable you to see His goodness and to focus on His purposes for you.

RESPOND :

. . . .

. . . .

. . . .

. . . .

. . . .

PLAN TIME

THINGS TO DO (3-5 MAX) :

KEY EVENTS TODAY :

MOVE TIME

MORNING WATER ☐

B : _____
L : _____
D : _____

SNACK :

SIMPLE WORKOUT ☐

WEEK 6, DAY 1: ESTHER 9:11-15

IT'S GOOD ENOUGH, *I shouldn't ask for more. God has already done so much for me.* Have you ever had these thoughts? Instead of going to God in prayer, have you ever believed the lie that He doesn't want to do more for you? Or maybe you've had prayers that expect a wish-granting-genie to answer instead of an all powerful, loving God. You know what I mean: *Lord, please give me that raise. The extra cash would be awesome.* Or maybe: *Please just make my kids be quiet, they are so embarrassing.* Both types of prayers are wrong, and here in Esther we see a request that is in stark contrast to how many of us, myself included, often pray.

When Esther was asked by her husband the king, "What further is your request?" she didn't bashfully say, "Oh I couldn't ask for more." No, she asked for complete victory over her enemy. What sticks out to me the most is that her request begins with "If it pleases the king..." She was bold with her request, yet wanted nothing more than he was willing to give. Her request reveals her respect for him; so much respect that she wanted her desires to match his desires. She only wanted what would please him.

I have to confess that my prayers aren't always as bold and respectful as Esther's. While I know that God desires that I have victory in my life, I often fail to ask for it. Or instead of praying for victory and freedom from my sin, I ask for things that will simply make my life easier or more comfortable, not considering what would actually please Him.

Jesus said *"Whatever you ask in my name, this I will do"* (John 14:13-14). He wasn't giving us unlimited wishes, He was encouraging us to ask for the things that bring glory and honor to His Father. We have a far greater relationship with our King than Esther did with King Ahasuerus; knowing this, we can trust that we can come boldly to His throne with our requests. We should do so frequently, with requests that will bring Him glory and honor—trusting that these same things reveal the victory He has won for us.

Lord in heaven, please teach us each to pray in a way that is pleasing to you. Show us how to make requests that bring glory and honor to your Son. Forgive us for praying in ways that don't. Amen.

— KEY VERSE —

And Esther said, "If it please the king, let the Jews who are in Susa be allowed tomorrow also to do according to this day's edict. And let the ten sons of Haman be hanged on the gallows." (Esther 9:13)

Hello mornings

God. Plan. Move.

READ : Esther 9:11-15
WRITE : Esther 9:13

REFLECT :
- What is significant about the words *"If it please the king"* in verse 13?
- How could the words "If it pleases the King" change the way you pray?
- Read John 14:12-14. What does it mean to pray in Jesus name?
- Consider how, when, and why you make prayer requests. How are your requests similar or different from Esther's?
- Write out a prayer asking the Holy Spirit to teach you to pray. Use "If it pleases the King."

RESPOND :

PLAN TIME

THINGS TO DO (3-5 MAX) :

KEY EVENTS TODAY :

MOVE TIME

MORNING WATER ☐

B : _____
L : _____
D : _____

SNACK :

SIMPLE WORKOUT ☐

WEEK 6, DAY 2: ESTHER 9:16-22

THINK ABOUT THE LAST TIME you spent a ton of energy to accomplish a goal. Maybe it was preparing a vegetable garden or perhaps if was several late nights studying for an exam. Maybe you have spent several hours in childbirth. Perhaps you've even spent time in the military and have seen hand-to-hand combat as the Jews did. When you were finished, you were most likely exhausted and wanted some down time—some rest.

There were a few words and phrases that stuck out to me as I read today's passage: rest, feasting and gladness, celebration, sending gifts, and joy. What do these things have in common? We often do these things when we achieve a difficult goal. We don't just celebrate any little thing, we celebrate the big things. And that's just what the Jewish people did. They enjoyed their victory over their enemies.

In verse 22, I am reminded of the Jew's initial sorrow and mourning when they heard Haman's plot to annihilate them. They wept, lamented, and lay in ash and sackcloth (Esther 4:1-3), but more importantly they had spent time praying and fasting (Esther 4:16-17). I admit that fasting is a bit of a mystery to me. I don't know exactly how it works or why God responds to it the way He does. But He does respond and He expects us to fast (Matthew 6:16). Why? Fasting is our way of letting go of what we physically need in order take hold of Who we spiritually need. Through this, our relationship with our Father deepens and we see new levels of victory and freedom in our lives.

The Jewish people rested, celebrated, and feasted. They experienced gladness and joy. They gave and received gifts because they accomplished their goal—they defeated their enemy. However, I submit to you the most important event leading up to their victory was not the physical battle itself. The most important part, the most vital and crucial thing that they did was to fast and pray. And they did this before they ever lifted a finger against their enemy. Strongholds break when we fight the spiritual battles first; when we take our needs to God and trust that He will provide, protect, and defeat.

Lord in heaven, thank you for the gifts of prayer and fasting. Thank you for listening and responding. Teach us to pray and fast even though we may never know exactly how or why it works. Help us to trust you with the battle and the victory. Amen.

— **KEY VERSE** —

...as the days on which the Jews got relief from their enemies, and as the month that had been turned for them from sorrow into gladness and from mourning into a holiday; that they should make them days of feasting and gladness, days for sending gifts of food to one another and gifts to the poor. (Esther 9:22)

Hello mornings
God. Plan. Move.

READ : Esther 9:16-22
WRITE : Esther 9:22

REFLECT :
- Do a word study for the word rest in verse 22.
- How and when can we experience rest after a battle?
- How does going to battle in prayer and fasting honor God? How does it show trust in Him?
- What does the Bible say about prayer? See Philippians 4:6, John 15:7, and Jeremiah 29:12.
- What does the Bible say about fasting? See Joel 2:12, Matthew 4:2-4, 6:16-18, and Acts 14:23.

RESPOND :

PLAN TIME

THINGS TO DO (3-5 MAX) :

KEY EVENTS TODAY :

MOVE TIME

MORNING WATER ☐

B : _____
L : _____
D : _____

SNACK :

SIMPLE WORKOUT ☐

WEEK 6, DAY 3: ESTHER 9:23-28

WHEN I PLAY BOARD GAMES WITH MY KIDDOS we usually each take a turn rolling a die to see who gets to go first. It's a mini game of chance before the actually game begins. And playing a not-so-mini game of chance is what Haman did when he had cast Pur, or lots, to determine the day he planned to destroy the Jews (Esther 3:7, 9:24).

What Haman did not understand is that he maintained no one's lot. Psalm 16:5 tells us that the Lord maintains our lot:

The Lord is my chosen portion and my cup;
you hold my lot.

Because God has total control of our past, present, and future, we do not need to worry about the seemingly random circumstances of our lives. He has it all under control even when things seem out of control.

The Israelites committed to celebrating yearly their victory over Haman and those that would kill them. They called this celebration Purim to remember that even though Haman had cast the lots to determine their destruction, he wasn't able to make it happen. Though Haman had the authority and power to make his evil schemes a reality, God had other plans. God held—and still holds—the lot of His people. God was on their side and Haman was unable to follow through with his plan.

When we find ourselves facing enemies or situations that seem undefeatable, when it looks like someone else is calling the shots—or casting the lots—we can remember that God is ultimately in control. We can pray and praise Him for the victory that will come. We can trust that our faithful God maintains our lot and works all things to together for our good (Romans 8:28). While God's best for us may not always include the easiest physical circumstances, His good will always be our physical, eternal best—being more like Jesus—the One who trusted God and went to the Cross for our ultimate good.

Lord in heaven, you are sovereign and knowing this brings me peace and joy, and gives me reason to celebrate. I praise you for being in control and working all things together for my good. I trust you with every circumstance of my life. Help me to trust you even more. In Jesus name I pray. Amen.

—  KEY VERSE —

The Lord is my chosen portion and my cup; you hold my lot. (Psalm 16:5)

Hello mornings

God. Plan. Move.

READ : Esther 9:23-28
WRITE : Psalm 16:5

. . . .

. . . .

REFLECT :
- Pray Psalm 16 out loud.
- Study the word *lot* from Psalm 16:5 and the word *purim* from Esther 9:26.
- Why is it important to understand Who maintains our lot?
- Read Romans 8:28-29. Based on the context, what is the "good" we are promised there?
- Purim was established to reflect on the Israelites' victory over their enemies. Why is it important to reflect on the victory Jesus won for us at the cross?

RESPOND :

. . . .

. . . .

. . . .

. . . .

PLAN TIME

THINGS TO DO (3-5 MAX) :

KEY EVENTS TODAY :

MOVE TIME

MORNING WATER ☐

B : _____

L : _____

D : _____

SNACK :

SIMPLE WORKOUT ☐

WEEK 6, DAY 4: ESTHER 9:29-32

THE JEWISH PEOPLE HAD JUST BEEN THROUGH A GREAT ORDEAL. They could have been eliminated from all of King Ahasuerus' 127 provinces. If Haman's plan had been successful, not a single Jew would have lived from India to Ethiopia. But God intervened.

Generations earlier, God made a promise. To Abraham, the father of the Jews, He had said, *"I will make you a great nation; I will bless you and make your name great; and you shall be a blessing. I will bless those who bless you, and I will curse him who curses you. And in you all the families of the earth shall be blessed"* (Genesis 12:2-3). God has faithfully kept that promise. Even today He intervenes as He sees fit for His people, staying true to His word.

It was said earlier in this study that God's name is not mentioned in the book of Esther, however, His presence is obvious throughout. His faithfulness to His people continued through each page of the story. And though the author doesn't specifically say it, I'm sure the purpose of Purim was to remember God and all that He had done for the Jews. Esther and Mordecai did not want God's intervention and victory to be forgotten.

God doesn't forget His people; this includes those who have been adopted into His family by faith in the saving power of Jesus. When God said, *"in you all the families of the earth shall be blessed,"* He was speaking of Jesus. Jesus is every family's ultimate blessing. When we find ourselves in the middle of a great ordeal that threatens to ruin us, we can trust the promises of God. Just as God ensured victory for the Jews, through the cross He has ensured victory for us over sin. God is faithful—always faithful!

No matter what we face on this earth—financial troubles, family drama, sickness, religious persecution, or the like—God has already ensured our victory. The sorrows and miseries of this earthly life cannot compare to the blessing of Jesus Christ Himself. When the final trumpet blows we shall be changed, will be raised incorruptible, and we will no longer feel the sting of sin (1 Corinthians 15:50-58). Jesus has won!

Lord in heaven, you are ever victorious and faithful! Thank you for intervening on our behalf and sending your Son to be our ultimate blessing. Help us to remember and celebrate all that Jesus has done and continues to do on our behalf. In Jesus name. Amen.

— KEY VERSE —

But thanks be to God, who gives us the victory through our Lord Jesus Christ.
(1 Corinthians 15:57)

Hello mornings
God. Plan. Move.

READ : Esther 9:29-32
WRITE : 1 Corinthians 15:57

REFLECT :
- Read Genesis 12:1-3. List several ways that the Lord has kept his promise in these verses.
- Read 1 Corinthians 15:50-58. What happens during our final victory?
- How do Genesis 12:1-3 and the story of Esther help you believe the promises in 1 Corinthians 15:50-58?
- List any biblical promises that you have witnessed God keep in your life.
- Write a prayer thanking and praising God for being faithful and victorious.

RESPOND :

PLAN TIME

THINGS TO DO (3-5 MAX) :

KEY EVENTS TODAY :

MOVE TIME

MORNING WATER ☐

B : _____
L : _____
D : _____

SNACK :

SIMPLE WORKOUT ☐

WEEK 6, DAY 5: ESTHER 10:1-3

GOD DOESN'T LEAVE THINGS TO CHANCE. While He does allow us our free will and the responsibility to make choices within our lives, He is fully sovereign and able to work all things together to fulfill His will (see Psalm 16 and Romans 8:28). It doesn't matter how many kings or Hamans, Esthers or Mordecais there are in the world, God is in control. How we choose to acknowledge and respond to His sovereignty is important. Whether or not we choose to honor and obey Him is crucial.

Esther and Mordecai both chose submission and obedience. Even though they had been raised to positions of prestige and power, they fell on their knees to pray and to fast. And it was through these acts of humility they were given direction, courage, and the boldness to obey God even when it seemed their enemy had the upper hand.

Esther and Mordecai could have easily sought and found security within the palace had Haman's plan not been counteracted. Had the massacre taken place, Esther and Mordecai could have simply remained within the palace walls safe and sound. It is unlikely that anyone would have attempted to lay a hand on them—the queen being the king's beloved and Mordecai being her respected father-figure. However, they did not simply use their positions of authority for their own benefit. They used their authority to serve and seek the *"good of his people"* (verse 3). They set aside their comfort and risked punishment in order to serve others (see Esther 4:11-5:1).

It is most likely that you, too, have some measure of authority in your life. For example, I have authority over my own children and the elementary students that I teach in my classroom. You may have authority in a women's ministry at church or over others at your place of work. Just as Esther and Mordecai did, the Lord wants us to use our authority to serve others; however, being able to do this doesn't happen without prayer. We need to spend time on our knees seeking direction, courage, and the boldness needed to seek the good of others and magnify the name of Jesus.

Lord in heaven, please enable me to use any authority in my life for the good of others. Use me as a conduit of your grace, peace, and love. If I have selfishly misused any authority, please forgive and cleanse me. Teach me to seek the good of the people in my life. In Jesus name. Amen.

— **KEY VERSE** —

For Mordecai the Jew was second in rank to King Ahasuerus, and he was great among the Jews and popular with the multitude of his brothers, for he sought the welfare of his people and spoke peace to all his people. (Esther 10:3)

GOD TIME

READ : Esther 10:1-3
WRITE : Esther 10:3

. . . .

. . . .

REFLECT :
– Read Esther 4 again. What did Esther risk to serve others?
– List the ways Mordecai "sought the good of his people" throughout the book of Esther?
– Read Matthew 20:28 and Philippians 2:7-8. How did Jesus use His authority to serve us?
– What authority do you possess? How have you used it? For yourself or others? How could your actions and attitude be different?
– Say a prayer seeking direction, courage, and boldness to obey God's plan for your authority.

RESPOND :

. . . .

. . . .

. . . .

— PLAN TIME —

THINGS TO DO (3-5 MAX) :

KEY EVENTS TODAY :

— MOVE TIME —

MORNING WATER ☐

B : _____
L : _____
D : _____

SNACK :

SIMPLE WORKOUT ☐

CONCLUSION

ISN'T OUR SOVEREIGN GOD AMAZING? As we've walked through the Book of Esther, we've seen the hand of Providence actively moving for the benefit of His people. We've looked at both Esther's and Mordecai's obedience and the victory of a people doomed to destruction. Without God, their situation would have been hopeless! And we've seen that even though God's name isn't mentioned in the book, He is definitely the main character at work behind the scenes.

God still is (and always will be!) the main character in life. What a marvelous and beautiful thing! Friends, the God of the entire universe cares about us immensely. He cares equally about the huge details of history and the small things in each of our lives. And if we ask Him to open our spiritual eyes, I believe He'll help us see His loving presence at work. He is ever with us and ever pouring out His love!

Sisters, I pray that God has used the story of Esther and the words in this study to bless you and draw you close to Him. When you close this book and walk away, I pray that you'll see a bit more of His plan for you. I leave you with these words of Peter the Apostle in 2 Peter 3:18, that you may *". . .grow in the grace and knowledge of our Lord and Savior Jesus Christ. To him be the glory both now and to the day of eternity. Amen."*

May we be like Esther, faithful and determined to do whatever it is that God has called each of us to do. When He calls, let's answer with her words, *"Then I will go."* (Esther 4:16) May we all walk together in obedience and victory, more aware of God's providence!

In Him,

Ali

ABOUT THE AUTHORS

ALI SHAW can't believe how blessed life is! As a Central Texas wife, momma, and new grandma, Ali leads a full, grace-filled life. She serves as the HelloMornings Bible Study Director and owns and writes for *DoNotDepart.com* and is generally in awe that God will use a regular girl like her! Woven with practical insight, her writing encourages women to seek God daily through the reading and study of His Word. Most of her writing can be found through HelloMornings or DoNotDepart, but she blogs occasionally at her personal blog, *HeartfeltReflections.wordpress.com* where she's written an online Bible study, Learning from Job. She has also authored an in depth Bible study of Abigail. For information or encouragement, you can connect with her on Facebook at *facebook.com/heartfeltreflectionsblog*.

For **COURTNEY COHEN,** everything comes down to two questions: Who is God? And, who has He designed us to be? Whether she's writing, speaking, or homeschooling her children, these questions propel her forward. Author of multiple books, including Refining Identity, Courtney passionately pursues helping others come to know God— the "I AM"—as their closest Friend. She also shares her testimony of living with type 1 diabetes in ever-increasing victory and healing in her book, Chronic Healing. Courtney is married to Steve, her most radical supporter, who also keeps her real. They have three children who, simultaneously, bless her socks off and keep her on her toes. Stay in touch with Courtney at IAM.NowFound.org, on Facebook at *www.facebook.com/IAmNowFound*, or on Twitter *@CourtneyLCohen*.

JAIME HILTON is $\frac{1}{6}$ of the Hilton Family in Lancaster, Pennsylvania. She is the household manager and wife of Ray, the actor. Together they are in the trenches of parenting three children, ages 5-11 with another expected this summer. Thanks to homeschooling and her voracious reading habits, she has her library card number memorized. In her (rare!) spare time, she likes to write and work with local theater companies, directing and encouraging fellow artists to glorify God in every aspect of their work. Her favorite mornings start with a quiet cup of coffee and an inspiring book or blog. Her most passionate pursuit is studying the Word and discovering the

stories within The Story. She blogs from time to time about life, homeschool, and theater at *classichiltons.wordpress.com* and is active on Facebook *@jaime.hilton*.

KELLI LAFRAM is actually Kelli LaFramboise, but no one can pronounce that, so with the permission of her hubby and four kids she writes under the shorter pen name. Her neighbors have started to referring to her bunch as the LaFram Fam. In addition to writing for Hello Mornings, Kelli has also led bible studies in her home and served in the children's ministry at her local church. Kelli is also an elementary school teacher and her hobbies include blogging about God's word, listening to audiobooks with her children, drinking good coffee, hand painting faith-based signs (but not after too much coffee), and helping her carpenter husband build furniture. You can find her at *www.quietlyreminded.com*, *https://www.facebook.com/KelliLaFram/*, and *https://www.instagram.com/kellilafram/*.

KELLY R. BAKER is a Bible study teacher, writer, mentor, and the founder of the Blogger Voices Network *https://kellyrbaker.com/blogger-voices-network/*. She serves with her husband in leading the worship ministry at their church. You will probably find her sneaking a bite (or more) of organic dark chocolate in between wrangling her four homeschooled kids. Her greatest passion is helping women thrive in Christ and keep a D.A.I.L.Y. T.I.M.E. with God. Connect with her on her blog at *https://kellyrbaker.com* and on Facebook at *https://facebook.com/kellyrbakerdotcom*.

SABRINA GOGERTY lives with her husband and three children–two rambunctious boys and an inquisitive daughter, all six and under–in central Iowa. She is a farm wife who happens to live in town, with a love for baking, reading, coffee, and connecting with and encouraging others. Between home life, local church ministry, and leadership in Bible Study Fellowship and Mothers of Preschoolers, there's not much time for writing these days. But whether it's putting together something for an online group of women or collaborating for HelloMornings, God has always seen fit to bless her heart through the discipline and joy of writing. Sabrina has found that time spent in His Word is never wasted and has joyfully been a part of HelloMornings since April of 2015.

Made in the USA
Las Vegas, NV
29 October 2021